More praise for *Mom, They're Teasing Me*

"Once again Michael Thompson, Lawrence Cohen, and Catherine O'Neill Grace have reached into the hearts and minds of children and parents and given us deeply needed advice, reassurance, and good news. They show us how to deal with some of the most painful moments of childhood and, not only survive them, but thrive. Michael Thompson combines the knowledge and wisdom of a brilliant psychologist with the heart and love of an experienced parent. This much-needed book is a true gem."

—EDWARD M. HALLOWELL, M.D.

"Few parenting challenges compare to helping a kid cope with teasing or being left out. With empathy and understanding, *Mom, They're Teasing Me* gives parents age-by-age information and practical advice to guide and comfort kids through every stage of their so-called social lives."

—FREDDI GREENBERG,
editor in chief, *Nick Jr. Magazine*

"What a wonderful and helpful book. It is right on target dealing with a very difficult issue—one that all parents confront—in a truly sensitive and intelligent manner. Above all, Michael Thompson and Lawrence Cohen give answers— why it happens and what to do about it. I was really impressed by their ability to make helpful sense out of a truly difficult part of child-raising."

—ANTHONY E. WOLF, PH.D.,
author of *Get Out of My Life,
but First Could You Drive Me
and Cheryl to the Mall?*

Mom, They're Teasing Me

—■—

Helping Your Child Solve Social Problems

MICHAEL THOMPSON, PH.D.
and
LAWRENCE J. COHEN, PH.D.
with CATHERINE O'NEILL GRACE

BALLANTINE BOOKS • NEW YORK

A Ballantine Book
Published by The Random House Publishing Group

www.ballantinebooks.com

Library of Congress Control Number: 2004091098

ISBN 0-345-45011-6

Manufactured in the United States of America

9 8 7 6 5 4 3 2 1

First Hardcover Edition: August 2002
First Trade Paperback Edition: August 2004

Text design by Susan Turner

For Theresa, Joanna, and Will, my greatest teachers
—Michael

—█—

For Emma, with love
—Larry

—█—

For my mom, Lois Decker O'Neill, who listened
—Catherine

CONTENTS

Introduction: *It All Started When She Hit Me Back . . .* xi

1 **The Everyday Lives of Children:** *Normal Social Pain* 3

Case Studies
Learning Not To Worry 6
Finding Your Place, Finding Yourself 16

Questions & Answers
Mom, They're Teasing Me! 29
Learning to Share 33
Friendship Skills for Life 37
Have Faith in Development 44
Addressing a Social Skills Deficit 48
Embracing Imaginary Friends 55
Popularity and Power 61
A Perspective on Pain 65
When the Group Causes Trouble 69
A Matter of Style 72
When a Boy Falls Head over Heels 76
Trying to Buy Friendship 79

2 When Social Life is Scary: *Children at Risk* 84

Case Studies
The Case of the Aggressive Preschooler 93
Sitting Alone at the Tea Party:
   A Neglected Child 102

Questions & Answers
Learning Nonverbal Language 108
When a Child Is Sadistic 111
How Can Two Kids from the
   Same Family Be So Different? 116
Talking About Personal Hygiene 119
The Roots of Bullying 124
A Girl Gang 127
Cracking the Code of Silence 132
Too Thin 139
Helping Children Deal with a
   Difficult Peer 144
Coming to the Rescue 151
Removing the Kick Me Sign 154
No One Is Safe Unless Everyone Is Safe 158

3 At School and in the Neighborhood: *The Social World of Children* 162

Case Studies
Helping Outcasts Find a Home 169
Harassed out of School 179

Questions & Answers

Be a Parent, Not a Kid   190

A Boy Marches to the Beat of a Different
   Drummer   194

The Tattletale   197

The Only Black Girl in Kindergarten   200

Not-So-Innocent Bystanders   204

Win-Win Leadership   207

To Box or Not to Box   212

When the Bullies Are Winning   218

Widening a Child's Social Circle   221

When Other Families
   Don't Follow Your Rules   225

When a Parent Doesn't Know
   How to Help   230

The Power of Love   233

The Language of Put-downs   237

Saying Good-bye to School   240

The Kindness of Children   244

INTRODUCTION

It All Started When She Hit Me Back...

What exactly is a parent supposed to do when a child comes home from school in tears because of a teasing incident or a friendship disaster? What do you do when your daughter is obviously in need of help in a social situation—but, as upset as she is, she's even more distraught at the idea that you might call the other parent or the teacher? So she pleads with you, "Don't call, Mom, please don't. Oh my God, you'll just make it worse!" What do you do if your child isn't receiving any birthday party invitations? How do you talk to other parents—or should you talk to other parents—about the fact that the phone never rings for your child? And if you are a teacher, what exactly is your role in protecting children from rejection or dealing with overly powerful cliques? Do you know that there is a secret social underworld playing out in front of your eyes every day? How much can you do to change it? How much worry is too much? How can we separate our children's experiences from our own painful memories of teasing or rejection?

We wrote this book to help answer questions such as these, questions that parents, teachers, and other adults face on a daily basis—questions that we have been asked again and again as we have traveled around the United States and overseas, giving workshops for parents and consulting to schools. Wherever we go, we hand out index cards and ask our audiences to share with us their worries about their children or their students. We have gathered hundreds of these question cards over the years, and from those we have focused on forty of the most common—and the most compelling—in these pages.

We want this book to help you understand the painful challenges as well as the extraordinary joys of children's social lives. We are two psychologists who specialize in children; we also do troubleshooting in schools and run workshops for parents and teachers. In our experience, problems that kids experience in their social lives are some of the most painful problems of all. Why do we say that? We have seen more mothers weep over these issues than they do about any other childhood problem.

When a parent is weeping or seething with anger about something going on socially with his or her child, the only response in that moment is empathy. But when things cool off a little, we have found that it often helps to explain some things about child development, so we will describe some of the psychological discoveries that we have found most illuminating. But as parents ourselves, we have been humbled to realize that sometimes knowledge of psychology is not much help. As much as we want to help, we sometimes lack data. Sometimes a child doesn't tell us her true feelings about a situation, so we are working with incomplete information, or she tells us but gives an account that is slanted in one way or another. (We often refer to this bias in reporting events to us with the phrase "It all started when she hit me back.")

Much of the time it turns out that perspective is more important than knowledge. If you are a parent, you already know that perspective is the toughest thing to maintain in child rearing. We all marvel at the balanced parent, the parent who doesn't explode, the parent with the light touch, the parent who doesn't get overinvolved, the consummate stage manager who can invisibly create an environment in which children solve their own difficulties. We all want to be like that, but very often we're pulled into a situation prematurely, or we hang back too long.

Here's a quick example of how important it is to get a broader perspective on children's social experiences. Imagine a mom and a psychologist standing outside a school talking. They are watching her son play on the climbing structure with a bunch of other kids, mostly younger than he is. As the grown-ups chat and watch the play, her son starts being very rough and mean with the smaller children. The psychologist wonders if the mom is going to say anything to the boy about it. She doesn't. Then, suddenly, the smaller kids realize that there is only one of him and lots of them, so they gang up on him.

The mom leaves the conversation in midsentence and goes running over to protect her boy. She shouts at the other children for ganging up on one kid and for being too rough, and bundles her son into her arms. He starts to sniffle and whine a little bit. This is for her benefit, it seems, since he was totally fine before she ran over, even while the littler kids were beating up on him. In fact, the psychologist thought that the boy may have even liked the other kids ganging up on him, because it gave him a chance to fight them more aggressively.

Were the mom and the psychologist both seeing the same thing as they watched the scene on the playground?

Probably not. Parents tend to have a biased view when they watch children's social interactions. Usually we see our own children as the helpless, innocent victims and other children as the mean ones. But some parents actually have the opposite bias, always assuming that their own child is at fault in any conflict. Teachers, meanwhile, often split into two camps, some identifying with the underdogs and others identifying with the top bananas. Another reason we don't get a full picture is that we see the world through the lens of our own experience. If we were bullied and rejected a lot as children, we may be more likely to see that happening to our child, even when it isn't. Or, alternatively, we may not even notice it anymore, since we have become inured to it. In the case of the aggressive boy whose targets turned against him, it wasn't training as a psychologist that allowed a clear view of what was going on. It was just not being emotionally involved.

So one goal of this book is to help provide adults with a more complete picture, which takes into account the whole situation, or as much of it as we can possibly understand. That means seeing the roles of every child, the group as a whole, the parents, the school, and every other aspect of the system. You will see that we seldom peg some children as simply victims and others as simply bullies. The world we portray is not a black-and-white world, but one of complex interactions between the individual and the group. We try to take a systems approach to the social problems of kids.

Suppose a parent asks, "How can I teach my son better social skills so he will be accepted by his peers?" That is related to a common question from teachers, "How can I get my class to stop scapegoating this one boy?" Take another look at those two very different questions. Did you notice that they could actually be referring to the same child, but from very different angles? The child may lack social skills and be an irritant for the group; the group may have found its sense of mission in tormenting one child. If you are going to change this dynamic, it is important to address all facets of the system. The answers in this book will always try to balance the individual perspective with the group perspective.

One of the hardest jobs for parents is to acknowledge our children's pain while also keeping it in perspective. The most common difficulties of child rearing come when adults either can't face that their child is suffering or take that suffering too much to heart. To help the reader understand how serious children's social suffering may be, we have divided the book into three sections: normal social pain, children at risk, and school and neighborhood problems. We have done so to help the reader distinguish between the expected, inevitable social pain of childhood and the kind of social trauma that can totally crush a child's self-esteem.

Normal social pain is very real. But it doesn't have the danger of leading to serious mental illness or suicide or homicide. When our child comes running to us with hurt feelings, or slams the door to her room and cries all night into her pillow, we can easily lose sight of the fact that our child is not in serious peril, even if she is in a great deal of pain at the moment. At the same time, many parents tend to minimize the suffering associated with loneliness or rejection. We try to offer a balance between acknowledging pain and keeping it in perspective, between intervening when necessary and not worrying too much.

Normal social pain comes from the inevitable and nearly universal aspects of group life and peer interactions. Every child is teased, every child has a fight with a friend, everyone likes someone more than that person likes them. A child can't be expected to have too much perspective on that. After all, it may happen to everyone, but it only hurts when it happens to you or someone you love. Therefore we, as adults, have to remember that this normal social pain will pass, and that there is a tomorrow with the potential for friendship and acceptance.

For those children at real risk, however, the concerns are very different. We may not want to face that our child is mean, or has no real friends, or is scapegoated by the group. But the research in this area is very clear: Children who are systematically rejected or neglected or aggressive are at a much higher risk for dropping out of school, drug and alcohol problems, depression, criminal behavior, and even suicide.

In our discussions with parents and teachers, we usually hear two main approaches to the group life of children. One style is a hands off, kids-do-that-kind-of-thing approach. When that approach fails, the results are reminiscent of the horrible scenes in *The Lord of the Flies* when the children revert to the influence of primal and destructive group forces.

The other approach is for adults to engage in a great deal of hand-wringing, interventions, serious talks, punishments, and so on, trying to replace those negative group dynamics with something more positive. That approach often fails as well. We suggest an alternative: a focus on teaching good leadership and conflict resolution skills, which helps the popular kids learn to be benign instead of cruel, lower-status kids to stick up for themselves and find acceptance in the group, and the majority in the middle to take a moral stand against teasing, bullying, and cruelty. In addition, adults can't be embarrassed to talk about kindness, morality, or compassion. Indeed, we must talk to children about those things all the time.

Like our book *Best Friends, Worst Enemies*, this one is a collaborative work among two psychologists, Michael Thompson and Larry Cohen, and a children's book writer, editor, and former teacher, Catherine O'Neill Grace. In our earlier book, we blended our three voices into one. In this book, you will be hearing primarily from the two psychologists, and we will switch back and forth between the "I" voice and the "we" voice. Why? It's less confusing. Can you imagine going to a psychologist's office and encountering two psychologists in two chairs giving two sets of advice? What a nightmare that would be.

Answering questions in the "I" voice allows us to use our respective life histories and experiences. When Larry writes about his daughter, Emma, you need to know that the story comes from him, so we have made that clear. However, because we share a common point of view and have worked together to refine each other's responses, we decided not to sign the answers to the questions. A few biographical notes about the authors will make it clear where some of the stories you will read in this book originated.

Michael Thompson, Ph.D., lives in Arlington, Massachusetts, with his wife, Theresa McNally, and their two children, Joanna, age sixteen, and Will, age eleven. He is the co-author of *Raising Cain, Speaking of Boys*, and *Finding the Heart of the Child*. In addition to his speaking engagements across the country and around the world, he is the psychologist consultant at the Belmont Hill School, an all-boys school in Massachusetts.

Lawrence J. Cohen, Ph.D., is a psychologist living in Brookline, Massachusetts, with his wife, Anne Fabiny, and their daughter Emma, age twelve. He is the author of *Playful Parenting* and a regular columnist for the *Boston Globe* and *Nick Jr.* magazine. Before beginning his specialization with children, parenting, and play, he worked extensively with survivors of sexual assault and abuse and their families. He has also worked with criminals, including sex offenders and batterers, which has shown him the more dismal side of human interactions.

Catherine O'Neill Grace lives in Waltham, Massachusetts, with her husband, Don Grace, on the campus of Chapel Hill–Chauncy Hall School, where Don is the headmaster. Catherine is the author of numerous books for children, most recently *1621: A New Look at Thanksgiving*. For fifteen years she wrote a health column for middle-school children for the *Washington Post*.

For all three of us, listening to children and adults talk about their friendships and their group experiences is a powerful lesson in the joy and the suffering that seem always to walk hand in hand in people's lives. As parents and teachers, we would like to provide our children with opportunities for happy friendship and group experiences. But it doesn't work that way, of course. We cannot stop the seas from being stormy. We can only help see to it that all children set out in sturdy boats and have safe harbors to come home to. As much as possible, we want our children's friendships, their classrooms and neighborhoods, and our own homes to be those safe harbors.

Mom, They're Teasing Me

1

THE EVERYDAY LIVES
OF CHILDREN:
Normal Social Pain

Every morning when the buses pull up in front of an elementary, middle, or high school building, an extraordinary social drama unfolds. Most adults miss the importance of this opening act of the school day, because it is a daily theater, apparently so predictable that grown-ups are not alert to its intensity. But kids get off the bus with their minds geared not to Spanish, spelling, or computer class, but to seeing their friends. They're ready for the curtain to rise on the action of the day—for the conflict and connection of social life.

Children suffer when they are teased or excluded or have a fight with a friend—and parents suffer empathically right along with them. Our job is to bear that pain and also to put it in perspective. After all, we lived through cliques and betrayals and heartaches, and our children will too. Of course, there are things we can do to ease the pain—theirs and ours—but our first job is to take a deep breath and trust in children's resilience and in the process of human development.

The social troubles children face are so predictable and inevitable that it is hard to call them traumas. Nevertheless, they do hurt and they do sap a child's confidence. Losing a friend, having a secret betrayed, and being teased are just a few examples. As parents, we want desperately to help children escape these hard lessons of life, or at least master them when they do happen. We know that lectures don't really work, but we keep giving them anyway, just in case. We aren't sure what else to do. We also know that our own endless worrying doesn't help, but we have a hard time turning it off.

Research shows that the majority of kids fall somewhere in the middle of the social hierarchy. Their status ranges from basically accepted to well liked to wildly popular. For these children, intense social issues (and pain) are still prevalent. In fact, pressures and conflicts are universal as kids deal with clashes among the individual, the friendship pair, and the group. Most of the answers to the questions in this section begin with reassurance. Our goal is to help adults understand such factors as temperament, group dynamics, and child development. Our hope is that a better understanding of these things will provide some perspective, a dose of optimism, and a little relief from the anxiety we feel. Parents and other adults all have their own painful memories of social struggles. These memories are triggered when children hand over their pain to their parents. It's hard to separate the new pain of your child's present from the old pain of your own school days. It's a bit like getting your toe stepped on when it's already broken.

When we label much of what you worry about as "normal" social pain, we do not in any way mean to trivialize it.

The pain we feel when we lose a loved one is universal too—and therefore "normal." But that does not lessen its sting. Nevertheless, knowing that something is universal, that you and your child are not the only people who ever went through this pain, can be powerfully comforting.

If you read between the lines as you look over the questions in this section, you'll see that more often than not, what parents and teachers are really asking is this: "Is my child normal?" "Are the children in my class normal?" There is often a great deal of anxiety and concern behind these questions. Much uncertainty and anxiety comes from a lack of experience about how normal it is for children to be in pain, or how normal it is for children to be so difficult for adults to understand and to handle. Normal children are not wonderful every minute. Their friendships aren't always a scene on a Hallmark card. In fact, they throw us all kinds of curve balls. I often share with parents this quote from the brilliant child psychiatrist D. W. Winnicott in his book *The Child, The Family, and the Outside World:* "What is the normal child like? Does he just eat and grow and smile sweetly? No, that is not what he is like. A normal child, if he has confidence in his father and mother, pulls out all the stops. In the course of time he tries out his power to disrupt, to destroy, to frighten, to wear down, to waste, to wangle and to appropriate. Everything that takes people to the courts (or to the asylums, for that matter) has its normal equivalent in infancy and early childhood (and in adolescence), in the relation of the child to his own home. If the home can stand up to all the child can do to disrupt it, he settles down to play; but business first, the tests must be made."

We have to bear the pain that our children share with us,

pain that might break our hearts or annoy us or remind us of our own horrible peer experiences. And we have to keep a sense of perspective about all that pain. Indeed, the first rule of worrying as a parent is to take the long view.

There is a story about an anxious first-time mother who called her baby's pediatrician constantly, sometimes several times a day. After a couple of months of this, he asked to see her. This is what he said: "Mrs. Smith, you have given birth to a child. You have opened yourself up to a lifetime of worry. You have to *pace* yourself." Kids, too, need to learn to pace themselves in the long-distance race of growing up.

In the first of the two case studies that follow, you will meet a mother who learned to manage her worry and to promote, rather than anguish about, her child's friendships.

The second case study in this section will introduce you to Karen, a young adult, and her reflections about the complex interplay of identity, friendship, and popularity during adolescence. Karen's ability to look back on her own social life helps her make sense of a struggle that was hard to understand when she was living through it. We hope her view will give you added perspective on your own children's experiences in the world of friendship and popularity.

CASE STUDIES

Learning Not to Worry

When Sandra talks about the ups and downs of her thirteen-year-old son Peter's friendships, she says things like this:

"You have to let things happen as they happen, without overreacting. But you also have to be there, ready to listen."

Sandra hasn't always been so philosophical about her son. A self-proclaimed worrier, she has spent a great deal of time thinking and agonizing about his friendships and his place in the group. But she has come to realize that she has to let her son make his own mistakes, suffer the bumps and bruises of childhood social life, and figure things out for himself—as anxiety-producing as that might be for her. She knows she can't protect him from these inevitable upsets, nor can she fix them all.

Still, she stays involved, believing that it is very important for her to be there to listen to Peter before, during, and after his time spent "figuring it out." All that listening helps her son solve problems on his own and helps her own peace of mind. Listening empathically—but not so empathically that it floods her with her own painful emotions—provides Sandra with an effective alternative to being overwhelmed and ratcheting up the anxiety level. She has learned to resist the temptation to jump in screaming and shouting about fairness or about who is being mean to whom.

At the same time, Sandra says that she works hard not to move too far in the other direction. She doesn't want to be so calm and relaxed about Peter's daily life that she ignores the real pain that her son and other children can feel as a result of their social encounters.

Sandra has discovered that the opposite of worry isn't necessarily calm serenity. When it comes to anxiety about our children's social world, the opposite of worry is trust. What Sandra has done over the course of thirteen years of parenthood is learn to trust her child—to trust his friendships and relationships and, most importantly, to trust in the process of development to sort things out.

It has taken Sandra some time to get where she is today. A few years ago, when Peter was nine, he came to her with a major upset about not being invited to a party by Ned, one of his best friends. Peter reported that Ned and some of the other boys in the fourth grade had been mean to him for several weeks. He didn't understand why they were being that way.

Sandra was devastated. As she realized later, she had an intense reaction because she was combining several layers of strong emotions. First was her empathy for her son, who was clearly in emotional pain. Second was her anger, that instinctive mama-bear protectiveness of her cub. Finally—and this is the most difficult and confusing layer—she had to deal with the way this event in her son's life reminded her of painful experiences in her own childhood.

All those layers of feeling contributed to Sandra focusing on the pain in the situation—her own and Peter's. She also was inclined at first to see her son as a helpless, innocent victim and the other boys as mean bullies. Such black-and-white thinking is a hallmark of reacting out of anxiety and worry, instead of reacting to a conflict or problem with trust and confidence.

Why is trust the opposite of worry? Because in Sandra's distress over this emotional upheaval, she forgot—temporarily—to trust in her son's resilience. Resilience is the ability to bounce back. Most children, Peter included, are remarkably resilient, even when they have suffered a serious upset or injury. Sandra also forgot her trust in the nature of friendships. They tend to go up and down, to cycle through conflict and turmoil. But friendships also tend to move back on track, or else the children move on to find other friends, putting the painful encounter behind them. Sandra also forgot for the moment about development. Nine-year-olds don't usually talk things out. They act them out, using the tools available to them—rejection, exclusion, teasing, and confrontation.

Fortunately Sandra did not just sit around stewing in her own juices, getting more and more anxious and angry. In the past she might have been preoccupied for a very long time with Ned's apparent rejection of Peter and the feelings it stirred up in her. She might have focused on her own old childhood memories of rejection and isolation. Instead, on her path from worry to trust, she looked for ways to manage her anxiety rather than escalate it. She had learned over the years not to focus primarily on her son's problems—an unfortunate but widespread parental tactic we call "interviewing for pain." So instead of asking Peter every day how it was going with Ned, she decided the best thing would be to get more balanced information.

So Sandra called Ned's mother, Bonnie. The phone call represented two big steps away from worry. First, Sandra had to trust that Bonnie would respond in a helpful way, that they could collaborate on understanding what was going on with the boys and help them work out a solution. Second, she trusted that the rift in the boys' friendship could be healed with a little work from her and the other parents involved.

The first thing Sandra learned, like every parent who has ever made this kind of phone call, is that there was more to the story than she heard from her son. From Peter's point of

view, Ned's cruelty and his failure to invite Peter to his party
came totally out of the blue—unexpected, undeserved, and
unprovoked. But it's never that simple, is it? When Bonnie
talked with Ned about it and called Sandra back, she added
a very different perspective. From Ned's point of view, Peter
was just getting what he deserved because he had done something at school to get a friend of Ned's in trouble. So that
friend had enlisted Ned and several other boys in a revenge
pact against Peter. But they didn't tell Peter why they were
talking behind his back, whispering at the lunch table, calling him a copycat if he said he liked what they liked, and saying he was uncool and wrong if he didn't like it. Peter had a
clean conscience about getting this other boy in trouble. He
thought he was just being a good citizen. He didn't put two
and two together, so he was puzzled by the mistreatment by
his former friends.

As Sandra and Bonnie talked, they realized that there
was another important factor involved. Ned was going to be
leaving the school where he and Peter had been together for
four years to attend a different school in the fall, although the
boys would still live in the same neighborhood. It was no coincidence that the hostility between the boys began right
around the time that Ned's family decided he would be
switching schools. The upcoming change helped both moms
understand why an invitation to Ned's party was so important to Peter.

Sandra got a lot more than information from her phone
call to Bonnie. She got a much broader perspective. She got
a picture of her son's role in the conflict, so she didn't have a
simplistic (and inaccurate) picture of him as a poor innocent
victim. She got empathy from her friend about her son's

rejection, and about her own feelings about it. She got an ally in her goal of rebuilding and restoring the friendship.

Furthermore, Sandra was able to see Ned as a child struggling with a difficult social issue of his own—leaving his old friends and making new ones—instead of as a mean kid who just wanted to hurt her own child. She realized that, like most people, Ned was having a hard time dealing with an upcoming loss. It made much more sense that Ned would pick fights with his best friends so that he wouldn't be so sad to leave them. Sandra was also able to realize that Ned was probably doing this with most of his friends, but that her son Peter might be especially sensitive to the dynamic of someone pushing people away so that a separation doesn't hurt so much.

Sandra obtained helpful information by looking outside herself and her son for different perspectives on the incident. She trusted that a more complete picture is a more accurate picture. She also used her husband and her friends as reality checks. As she says, "If you tell people what happened and they all act like 'What's the big deal?' then that's a pretty good sign that all the worry is an overreaction. Usually it means that the worry is a leftover feeling from my own childhood, instead of a fitting response to the current situation. But if other people are also worried, or they see that it makes sense to worry or be angry, then that helps me trust my instincts and my feelings that there is a real problem that I should be worried about."

Because she knew his friendship with Ned was important to Peter, and because she realized that Ned wasn't an evil monster, Sandra made a special effort to get the two boys together in a fun setting. She kept it low-key, trusting that just having some time together was all they needed to get things back on track.

This was another big step in trust for Sandra. In the past she would have come across very strongly, fussing at Ned for being mean to Peter or asking him forcefully what was going on. On the other hand, part of her balancing act was not to leave things entirely alone. She knew that if she did nothing, the two boys might well drift apart—and she knew that Peter, and probably Ned too, would regret that. She avoided both of the most extreme reactions—verbally attacking Ned or encouraging Peter to end the friendship, and just letting things slide. Instead, she actively encouraged and facilitated the healing of the friendship. She trusted instead of worried, believing this time that if parents can get children together, proximity will heal the rift.

Most psychologists who work with parents frequently find themselves saying, "Don't worry." Some people just need a little reassurance that their child is normal or that they haven't wrecked everything. But of course, no one can just snap his or her fingers and stop being anxious. The real goal is to manage the anxiety, to channel it into constructive avenues. Sandra continues to get anxious but does a much better job managing her anxiety now than she used to.

How does she do it? "When Peter tells me something or I see something that really bothers me, I manage my anxiety by working with myself, trying to find a balance between overreacting and overresponding versus pulling away and just being annoyed by it or ignoring it. A large part of this is recognizing what part of my reaction is from my own past— which was definitely not good in terms of peer stuff, especially in middle school. That's often the source of the intensity of my emotional reaction, so if I just respond out of that feeling, it's usually not very helpful," she says.

A recent event signaled a big turning point for Sandra. Once again it involved not being invited to a party—but this time the emotional aspects were different for both Peter and Sandra. Peter is generally well liked, with plenty of friends. But rejection is very painful for him, and his mom, when it does happen. This time Peter was not invited to a sleepover that most of the other boys at his usual lunch table crowd were invited to. He was very upset.

Sandra's first response was different from her overly worried reaction when Ned rejected Peter. This time she responded by saying that this wasn't such a big deal. After all, he and the boy having the party weren't such close friends, and the boy probably had a limit to the number of kids he could invite over. Sandra was kind of proud that she had managed not to overreact.

But before she could pat herself on the back, she realized that Peter felt criticized and invalidated by her reaction. He was already feeling bad about himself for caring so much and being upset by the rejection. At age thirteen, he thought, he should be able to let it roll off his back. But he couldn't; it really got to him. His mother's suggestion that he not blow it out of proportion echoed his own feelings of inadequacy about not being able to take it in stride.

"I should have just validated his disappointment," Sandra said. "It's taken me a long time to learn that the best thing to say is just, 'I see you're upset. I can understand why you'd be sad about it. You really wanted to go.' Stuff like that. At least I've learned to ask him for his ideas of what he wants to do about it, instead of leaping in with a million suggestions.

Eventually we settled on a plan for the weekend where he would do some fun things he wanted to do, and he felt better. In fact, I think he got over it before I did. But I've been thinking about this incident with the sleepover a lot. It illuminated something for me that I hadn't realized, which is that when I work hard not to panic and make a situation into a crisis of my own, I can go too far in the other direction and say it's no big deal. But for him it *is* a big deal—it's just not as big a deal as I sometimes make it out to be when I add on my own old feelings about rejection or exclusion."

Once again, the opposite of worry is trust—trust that there will be other sleepovers and, for Sandra, another chance to "do it right" and strike a balance between confidence and empathy. Sandra has learned not to turn every little incident into a catastrophe. She no longer sees a conflict with a friend or exclusion by the group as permanently damaging to Peter.

Sandra seems to be well on her way to finding that balance she's been seeking. The other day when Peter came home and said another boy put him down because he isn't as talented athletically as that boy is, she didn't spin out of control with her worry and her protectiveness. And Peter has matured too. Instead of falling apart as he used to, which only fed Sandra's worry more, Peter told her, "We just don't get along. It's no big deal—let it go." Peter was annoyed by the incident but not overwhelmed emotionally. And Sandra was disappointed but not devastated, as she would have been in the past. Why not? She says it's because of the internal work she has done to untangle her own past from her son's present.

The other big change is that Sandra and Peter talk more

about social strategies he's tried and those he'd like to try next. Even when those strategies are not entirely successful, Peter is telling a different story than he used to, and Sandra is supporting that new story. Peter isn't telling a victim story—his old favorite. He is telling a more empowered story about what he tried to do to help things. And he's telling a more balanced story, acknowledging his role in conflicts. Sandra is more able to see things as a system too, and not simply as another example of her poor little boy being mistreated.

There has been a significant shift from worry to trust in the content of Sandra's mental activity, as well as a shift in its intensity. She still thinks a lot about Peter's friendships and about any teasing or exclusion he might be involved in—as victim or bully—and she still spends a great deal of mental energy on it. But there is less panic, less escalation, and more trust in Peter, Peter's friends, Peter's resilience, and Peter's maturity.

Most of all, she has a new, trusting attitude that this too shall pass. In the past she tended to see everything bad that happened through a veil of gloom and doom. Now if there's some pain or anguish, she figures it will end. If a friendship is going well, she doesn't set herself up for disappointment by fantasizing that the boys will be best friends forever, and then feel devastated when one of them is mean or things go awry. This too shall pass, because all friendships have ups and downs. And it really pays, she says, to keep in good communication with other parents, even if the kids are involved in a conflict or are in a downswing of their friendship. That way things don't escalate from a temporary conflict to a permanent rift. And keeping in touch with the other parent, like her phone call to Ned's mom, helps Sandra avoid writing off a kid who is mean to Peter. This too shall pass—and in four months they might be good buddies again.

Sandra now trusts that not everything has to be perfect in Peter's friendship and group life. Instead of seeing the end of the world in any setback, conflict, or mean word, she realizes that "a boy will be okay if he has a couple of good friends—and Peter does." Another shift is that when there is a problem between Peter and his peers, Sandra now sees it as her job to help him heal from it. That's a big change from feeling that she had to protect Peter at all costs, to get to the bottom of things, and, most urgently, to somehow stop her own pain and panic by fixing the situation. Instead of leaping in with both barrels blazing to stop one person from picking on another, she sees a system that needs a little help. Or maybe she just needs to do some empathic listening and some encouraging of Peter so that he can go back and try something new.

Finding Your Place, Finding Yourself

"Say you start out socially when you are three or four," said Karen. "At that point it's very democratic. Everybody likes everybody, and everybody plays with everybody. And then as you get older, people sort of, I don't know what the word is, but they isolate themselves into small groups, and that gets exponentially worse up through about seventh grade. That's probably the turning point, and at that point it starts to ease, just a little bit. Then through high school it eases a little more so that the groups are still there but the lines aren't as rigid. People don't feel the need to knock each other down in order for them or their group to be good. And then I think once you move into college you're way past all of that."

This eloquent capsule view of the progress of a child's social life comes from a recent college graduate. Young adults' memories of their childhood social situations remain fresh, even though they have moved on to another level of development. Their perspective on the social lives of children can be illuminating. Karen made it clear that she had given a great deal of thought over the years to what it means to find yourself and to find your place in the group—or outside the group.

The earliest memory Karen had of things not being "democratic" anymore comes from second grade. She and a friend were very upset that a girl named Lulu was acting like the queen of the world—or at least the queen of the girls on the playground. They were even more upset that all of the other girls were willing to go along with her coronation.

"She was walking around the playground at recess and there were seriously ten or fifteen girls, like a line of ducks, following her to wherever she decided to go to play," Karen recalled. "Looking back, I can say, 'Poor Lulu.' But my friend and I decided we wanted to play somewhere else. It's not that easy, though, is it? When you're that age you can't just break away from the pack and go play by yourself, so we decided to tell the teacher. Because it seemed like a fairness thing, we decided we were going to tell the teacher that it wasn't fair that Lulu got to decide where everyone goes. So we went over there and told the teacher, and she was like,

'Well, what can I do?' And I just couldn't believe it. I mean, it's moments like that where you kind of start to realize how things work."

Karen jumped from there to some specific experiences from middle school, which she called "the pinnacle of social cruelty." She recalled a period of wanting to be in the most popular group and being shut out. She remembers that it took her a while to get the hint. At first she believed the popular girls when they had some excuse not to come over or some reason why they didn't invite her over. Karen isn't really sure if this story counts as a traumatic experience. "I mean, that rates very low on the social trauma scale, I think. Part of the reason that I can give a good breakdown of how popularity works is that I always remained somewhat out of the fray. I was never at the epicenter of the popularity movement, nor was I ever ostracized or anything like that. People generally respected me for being smart and counted on me to know things and saw me as one of the smart kids, but not in a dorky way. That may have something to do with the fact that I went to a school that is very strong academically and we were taught to sort of respect that."

Young adults have vivid memories of their childhood and teenage social experiences, so they are wonderful sources of information about this period of development. However, a vivid memory is not necessarily a totally accurate memory. We forget things because they are too painful, or we reshape our memories to fit our perceptions of ourselves. To get some corroboration of Karen's memories, I interviewed her mother as well. Of course, parents forget and distort memories also, so it is very interesting to compare differences between two people's memories of the same set of events.

Karen's mother remembers Karen being much more upset by rejection than Karen herself does. Where Karen remembers having *chosen* a new group, and chosen to be something of an outsider, her mother remembers a period of significant distress. Perhaps Karen has forgotten that before those choices there was the sting of rejection. Her mother said, "She claims now that at school those girls were friendly and weren't mean to her and that she put *herself* on the outside by not dressing like them and not having the same interests, but I always felt, and her father always felt, that it was the other way around. I think she coped with the rejection by making her own way and becoming more of an individualist."

In fact, Karen's mother explained that because Karen was always very social and outgoing, middle-school rejection hit her very hard. In earlier years, popularity and friendship had overlapped. Having a close circle of friends meant being accepted in a group, and vice versa. But later the emphasis was on status and hierarchy within the group. Karen's mother remembers trying to help her with agonizing decisions about whom to invite to a sleepover, whom to call next if that person wasn't available, wondering what it meant if someone said no, and so on.

But Karen remembers this whole period as no big deal. How can we understand this difference in memory? Is it that Karen has buried the painful memories? Or has she reframed those memories in light of her current sense of identity? Maybe it's her mother's memory that is distorted. Perhaps mothers take it to heart when their children are hurt, while the child heals from the experience and moves on. Probably the truth contains a bit of both.

In some areas, however, the memories of mother and daughter meshed perfectly, even though they hadn't talked about the incidents for years. Remember Lulu, the queen of second grade? Karen's mother remembers her as spelling trouble from way back in kindergarten. She said that at parent-teacher conferences, the topic would often turn to social issues because Karen's academic performance was not a problem. "Karen's teachers would describe Lulu as an instigator, telling some kids not to play with other kids, saying 'I'm not going to be your friend' and 'If you play with so-and-so I won't be your friend' and 'This is what you have to do if you want me to be your best friend today.' For the other girls it was kind of a love-hate thing. They loved Lulu and wanted to be close to her, but they resented her power. And apparently she got her comeuppance in high school."

One funny tangent to this story is that Lulu's mother and Karen's mother went to school together, where Lulu's mother was also a social leader. Karen's grandmother even remembers Lulu's mother at age eleven getting all the other girls to sneak off and get their ears pierced.

As Karen and her mother talked, one theme kept emerging—the conflict between individuality and being part of the group. Karen said, "Elementary school and middle school are hard for anyone who has a sense of individuality. Lots of kids don't, and they feel safe because there is a group. Even if they're in the dork group, at least they are in a group. Individuality is not rewarded or encouraged by the social regime. It may be encouraged by parents and teachers, but that's irrelevant at that age. The group rules."

She described more about how this tyranny of the group operates, especially in middle school: "Being smart is good, but being really, really smart is not good. And the same thing for being pretty. Being pretty is good for popularity, but if we'd had someone who was drop-dead gorgeous, a future supermodel, she would have been outcast too. Standing out in any way is not tolerated.

"So like I said, I had some element of popularity from being smart, but as I got older I tried to temper this, so it wouldn't go over onto the too-smart side. In seventh grade, when we took these tests, me and this socially retarded boy were the only ones who got high enough scores to go to this special ceremony. I said, 'Over my dead body. I will jump in front of a bus before I go to that.' Of course the other kid went. Good grades and high test scores were all he had, I guess, and that's what was totally important to him.

"In high school, at least in my high school, it was different, because academic achievement was valued. So you went up in status if you were real smart, but still, the kids at the epicenter of popularity were never the smartest kids. They were maybe solid B averages. You'd be surprised if a super-popular kid was on the honor roll."

Speaking of the honor roll, Karen's mother remembers a conversation they had when Karen was in sixth grade and about to get her first report card. Karen told her mother that she was worried about getting high honors and getting her name posted on the big list by the front door of the school. Karen said she was even considering talking to the principal about not being posted, because she didn't want to be perceived as a brain or a nerd. As her mother recalled, "Up until that report card, she had been thrilled to get very good grades. But all of a sudden those grades had a social meaning. A negative social meaning. Karen told me—close to tears, if I remember correctly—that she had already been pegged as a goody-goody whom all the teachers liked and who was good at everything, the one who always got the A-plus when there was only one A-plus in the class. She said she decided not to talk to the principal because if her name wasn't on the list, people would think she hadn't even made the lowest level of honors."

Karen's mother could empathize with her daughter about this dilemma, of wanting to do well in school but not wanting it to be publicly displayed, inviting resentment and jealousy and a label as Miss Perfect. "I tried hard in school myself to not be dorky, even though I got good grades. I think that's why I remember this so well. We had a good discussion about how this wasn't exactly 'teasing'—it was more like being pegged as a certain kind of person, and then that is the shorthand used to identify you and talk about you. I wanted her to notice that everyone gets one of these pegs, and they generally have a negative cast to them, so that no one gets too far ahead of the pack. These pegs are a lot like stereotypes in that they narrow a person down to one characteristic, boy-crazy or goody-goody or hyper or whatever. But of course that doesn't help very much when you are eleven or twelve. So what if everyone else is being pegged? It's your own dilemma that really matters, being pushed into a box you don't fit into."

If Karen doesn't remember how traumatic it was to be excluded, she does remember being on the dishing-out end of the teasing and bullying dynamic. "At most schools I think you have these very delineated lines between the cool kids, the specific dorks that everyone teases, and everyone else in the middle. My school wasn't really like that. It was more like these are the people who count, and then these others are the nonexistent people. You know what I mean? It felt like there was not as much teasing as there was just total ignoring, which I think is almost harder for people, because it's as if you just don't exist. And I know I participated in that. I did not have whatever it must take to make friends with someone who is considered by the group to not exist. Looking back at that helps me understand what happened at Columbine. I don't think it was about the teasing. Teasing can make someone feel like a second-class citizen, it can make someone feel like a reject, but at least if you're teased you have something to fight against. But if you are ignored and you feel like you don't exist, what can you do? What you want is to prove to people that you exist. That, to me, is what they were saying. They weren't contradicting the fact that they were dorks. They weren't contradicting the fact that they were weird. They were contradicting the fact that these people, the jocks and cheerleaders and student council presidents, thought they didn't matter. And they were basically saying, 'Look how much we matter.' And you can't just write them off as crazy kids. You could probably go to any school and pick out a few people who are capable of that."

What does Karen think about her mother having such a different memory of the emotional impact of events? "I know that I never really felt like I was in the heart of anything, but that was also on purpose. I mean, I didn't want to be with them either. There were certainly times when I wished that I was, but for the most part it made me much more comfortable to be able to sit outside and observe while still being part of it enough. I've always been friends with those people, but I've never been in the coolest group, and in the end I think that really helped a lot with independence and the feeling of being free enough to make my own choices.

"When you hit high school a lot of those people aren't at the top of the heap anymore anyway, and that's a real eye-opener. I can give you one example. That girl Lulu, the one who was the queen of the world—I always thought that she was the most perfect person I had ever seen. But when we were in fourth grade her parents got divorced, and it was definitely one of the big revelations of my lifetime that no one's life is perfect, that no one is free from those kinds of things. And it's funny, because over the years she grew away from her original friends, who were still sort of the ruling members of the class, at least in a party sense, all through high school. She grew away from them and she really changed. I mean *really* changed. Like she and I are friends now and you know she's just very real, a very good friend.

"I look at her as a really good indicator of how high school can change things, so popularity isn't as important and friendship is. It's a change from being fake to being real, I guess. I think what it really comes down to is fear. Everybody is really afraid, and I think the reason that sixth grade and seventh grade are probably the hardest time socially is because it's also the hardest time personally. Because it's such a dynamic period of time for everyone. Everyone is changing at a different rate and is at a different point. But at the same time everyone is supposed to act the same and dress the same and look the same and like the same music. And when you put all those really uncomfortable people together, they are fighting tooth and nail to get the attention off them. You don't want somebody to look at you, so you say something so everyone will look at someone else."

Thinking back, Karen regrets some of the behavior she fell into during the social wars. "There was this girl who I was semi-friends with when I was in fifth and sixth grade, and I was hanging out with her and she told me that she shoplifted sometimes, and showed me some things she had stolen. I was pretty freaked out by this, and I could have just not said anything about it and just let it go. But I was too immature and I went and told all my friends and I acted all superior, and she got this big reputation as like, you know, a criminal and a bad kid. And that reputation lasted for another two years. We ended up being friends when we were older and she never brought it up, but I felt really bad. What I'm trying to say is that you get a kid like me—I think I've always been somewhat mature for my age and smart, but at that age even I wasn't capable of being a big person, you know? I couldn't put aside my own fear of being laughed at in order to do the right thing and keep a confidence."

One of the themes of this book, and of Karen's memories of her school-age social struggles, is the complex interplay between friendship and group life. Friendships at her school, Karen said, always had an edge to them, an edge that had to do with each person's social standing in the group. Here's how she described it:

"My school, I see now, had a strongly precocious social kind of environment where in kindergarten you were already preoccupied with who is hanging out with whom. It was sort of like the stock market. The stock market never stops going up and down, right? And the ups and downs are mostly just based on opinions. It's not as though this stock is high because this company makes a lot of money. This stock is high because people think it's going to be worth something. It's entirely based on opinion. And social systems when you are a child or when you are a preteen are the exact same way. Someone could fall out of favor and you don't want to be stuck with your pants down being friends with them. And for that reason there is no loyalty. There is no true friendship. There are people who are constantly trying to ingratiate themselves with the person who happens to hold the most power.

"Each person's personal stock goes up and down, and you don't want to be stuck holding the shitty stock. You want to sell before it falls. So people are not sitting there thinking, 'This is my friend.' They are thinking, 'Could I be friends with a more popular person? Could I be hanging out with a more popular person right now? Do I want to call up and invite this person to a sleepover at my house, or that person?' It's really not about friendship; it's about accumulating status points and not getting stuck with a loser."

Could friendship enter into it at all? Karen said, "Well, there's a certain level of bonding that's real. But here's an example. When I was in sixth grade, all summer I was really, really good friends with this one girl, and then school started and we just weren't friends anymore—she just kind of bailed out on me. And I had friends when I was younger that I would spend time with if there was no one else around, if there was no one else available. But I didn't really like them. Because it's like nobody wants to be stuck doing nothing on Saturday night. That's really what it's about. I'm not sure

really where parents come into that, because my memory of
my childhood—which may be skewed, obviously—is of my
mother constantly telling me I'd better make some plans for
the weekend: 'Did you make any plans for the weekend yet?'
Whereas I would have been content to not do anything, at
least sometimes. But she really pushed me to be very, very
social, so I was constantly calling people that maybe I wasn't
even friends with. So an invitation to sleep over becomes a
game and is not about who you really like."

Not surprisingly, Karen's mother remembers this somewhat differently. She does remember urging Karen to make
plans for the weekend, but from her perspective, that was
because Karen was distraught if she waited too long to make
plans and all the "good choices" were already taken. Karen's
mother did not see herself as pushing her daughter to be
more popular, but only as helping her not be devastated
by being left out. They both remember conflicts about the
idea of inviting someone back because they invited you. For
Karen's mother this was a simple matter of courtesy. For Karen
it was much more complex than that. She knew that her
mother did not understand the rules and regulations of who
could invite whom and what those invitations meant.

Fortunately, these issues subsided during high school.
Here's Karen's description of how that works: "I think what
happens is that you grow into yourself and start to appreciate your own individual traits, whereas in the beginning you
just want to fit in. The superpopular group still has a lot of
power when it comes to clothes and music and parties, but
everyone's figuring out who they really are. And that fosters
real friendship. It fosters a desire to have someone connect

with you. In middle school anything that makes you different is an albatross, and by the end of high school anything that makes you different is a virtue."

When the group rules, Karen said, you can't afford to open yourself up to people. "I mean, what I did about the girl who shoplifted is proof. This poor girl was taking a big chance confiding in me, and I blew it. And what's the lesson? Don't show yourself. The worst thing is everybody's scared. We're scared of growing up and all the boy-girl stuff and getting our periods, but you can't act like you're scared or you'll immediately be branded a loser. So you need to keep up with the social hubbub, which really just teaches you how to be fake and how to not talk about how you feel. I remember being in seventh grade writing these poems and once my teacher published one of them in the school literary magazine, and I lost it. I lost my shit. Because I was like 'Oh my God, everyone's gonna laugh at me. I don't want anybody to see that part of me. I don't want anybody to see the inside of me.' "

Does Karen have any advice for parents about all this social trauma? Her thoughts were very much in keeping with what we recommend throughout this book: "I think that basically, when your child is still young enough that they'll listen to you, you try to foster all the values that you care about. But you are not going to see them reflected until the kid is around fifteen. It's like a long-term mutual fund or an IRA account—you can't get your money out for a while, but you've made a good investment. That's kind of what my parents did, and I went through some serious shit, but I came out feeling good about myself. I came out reflecting a lot of the things that they taught me."

QUESTIONS & ANSWERS

Mom, They're Teasing Me!

Q: *I met the school bus the other afternoon, and instead of my usual bouncy and enthusiastic kindergartner, I picked up a weepy, trembling child who flung herself into my waiting arms. "Mom, they're teasing me!" she wailed. It turned out that some kids had called her a baby for bringing a beloved and battered stuffed toy to school. I was so upset that I wanted to jump onto the bus and smack all the other little kids. In fact, I'm still upset, even though now my daughter seems to have forgotten all about it! Please tell me—why are kids so mean?*

A: The pain of the moment you describe is hard to bear. Your daughter just discovered the power of the group to scapegoat her. You suddenly realized that your child ventured out there into the world and was subjected to the verbal slings and arrows of other children. And you were not there to protect her! That's a hard reality. Harder still is the deeper realization that this is only the beginning. You will face many other moments of helplessness and fury like this in the future. We know this because we all went to school too. When we were kids we knew very well how threatening other kids could be.

When our own child is attacked, it is as if we are rediscovering human evil. We react to how completely pointless it is for a child to be tormented because she has brought a stuffed toy to school. Who was hurt by it? Why does the group care? Why did they have to tease her about it? Their cruelty seems senseless, and so we cry out, "Why are kids so mean?"

Though at an emotional level I certainly understand why parents ask that question, at a philosophical level I am baffled by it. I want to shout back, "Why are adults so mean?" What about the Catholics and the Protestants in Northern Ireland? The Palestinians and the Israelis? The Taliban? And have you forgotten racism in the United States? Groups of human beings are capable of the most terrible mistreatment of one another. The history of humankind—and particularly of the twentieth century and the beginning of the twenty-first—is one of groups tormenting and dominating one another, of people singling out completely innocent people and killing them for no reason at all other than that they are "different."

Adult cruelty has its roots in childhood, and it must make its first appearance somewhere. At some point, very early on, children discover that they have social power over other children. Once they discover the edge that they might have over others, they start to experiment with it. Larger toddlers start to throw their weight around as young as two and a half, intimidating smaller kids. Four-year-olds test each other by teasing and seeing which child among them doesn't bounce back from the teasing. They sort out the criers that way. Your daughter has experienced firsthand the kindergarten phenomenon of children in a loose coalition discovering that they can tease one child for being a "baby."

Why do they do it? Is it because your daughter was so different from others that she brought a stuffed animal to school? No, not really. Everyone in kindergarten has a stuffed animal they care about. If the teacher had invited every child in the class to bring in their teddy bears, they would have been thrilled. There might have been a celebration of the entire toy-animal kingdom in the classroom. Instead, your daughter was teased for something that all children love.

What happened in your daughter's class was almost a random event. I can't know for sure, but perhaps a boy was made uncomfortable by seeing the stuffed animal because he had so recently given up the wish to be accompanied by his stuffed animal himself. Or perhaps an older brother or sister teased him about his attachment to his "blankie." Possibly his mother had to talk him out of taking his own favorite thing to school. Having been accused of being a baby by an older sibling, or persuaded to act more grown up than he actually felt, he saw your daughter with her stuffed animal and attacked her with much the same words he had heard himself. Perhaps he was a physically large boy and wanted to establish his credentials as the most powerful child in the classroom.

Maybe your daughter had the bad luck to come to the attention of a verbally precocious girl who wanted to make a social splash by belittling a classmate. Maybe that girl wanted to appear older and more sophisticated in front of the other children. She could have been a bossy critic, like Lucy in *Peanuts* or Angelica in *Rugrats*. ("You babies," Angelica always declares with contempt. "You're still in diapers!") One of the reasons that *Peanuts* has been successful for decades is that we all recognize Lucy. We knew her in school when we were growing up. (We still know her in adulthood. She lives down the street!)

Yes, but *why* is there a boy bucking to be the bully of

kindergarten? *Why* is there a bossy girl? Do all children wish to be bullies at one time or another?

No, they don't all want to be bullies—but at one time or another all children do yearn for power over others. They long to command the attention, respect, admiration, obedience, and love of others. We all had—and have—the wish to show 'em, to dazzle 'em, to frighten 'em, to inspire their awe. At one time or another all children compete for the applause of the audience composed of their classmates. Sadly, one of the ways to entrance that audience is to pick on a smaller, more vulnerable child in front of a crowd—and there's always a vulnerable child in kindergarten. The other day it was your daughter.

What can I say to comfort you? If it doesn't happen a second day, she will feel better and so will you. It isn't likely to be an everyday thing in kindergarten; the bullies are too young and the group too disorganized to pick on one child regularly. If your daughter finds a way to pay back her lead tormenter the week following her humiliation, that may persuade him or her that your child is not a passive victim. It isn't attractive, but it is effective, and most children find a way to even the score. Perhaps the healthiest thing your child can do is to forget it and move on to enjoy her kindergarten year. The natural resilience and happiness of children is a powerful antidote to teasing.

I hope the teacher intervenes and reinforces classroom rules of tolerance, inclusiveness, and respect for all children. I hope the teacher speaks about those virtues every day and that all of the teachers who follow that first kindergarten teacher do too. It is the moral clarity of teachers—and parental support for what teachers do—that makes class-rooms safe for all children. Every child is entitled to a psychologically safe classroom where it is okay to bring in a stuffed animal and expose all of the vulnerable feelings of human life.

Learning to Share

Q: *My toddler doesn't share very well. I don't want to be a worrywart, but I can't help thinking that he'll have trouble making friends if he doesn't learn to share.*

A: A toddler who has trouble sharing? Alert the media! Call out the cavalry!

Sorry to be sarcastic, but this is one area where parents worry endlessly—and usually needlessly.

Why do parents worry? Because we want our children to be moral and kind. We want them to be well liked. We also want the other parents to see what a great job we have done parenting our toddlers. Those are all reasonable desires, and it is indeed a good thing to be able to share.

So why give up worrying? Because development is on our side and generally takes care of this temporary problem. Virtually every child has trouble at first with sharing, and almost all of us get over it. Take the Dalai Lama, the leader of Tibetan Buddhism, widely regarded as among the most compassionate people on the planet. Like other lamas, when the present Dalai Lama was a young boy he was taken from his family and brought to the monastery to be raised in an atmosphere of pervasive spirituality. At first his brother was sent with him, for companionship, but they were later separated. Why? Because they fought so much! So much for wishing *our* children can transcend sibling rivalry or petty squabbles.

Sharing is a universal issue for toddlers because they are moving from a state of infancy, in which they depended on adults to meet all their needs, to a state of independence and autonomy. Their focus is on asserting themselves. As you undoubtedly know from experience, "No!" and "Mine!" are the most frequent words in this stage of development. At the same time, they become able to keep their attention focused for longer, so sharing or not sharing becomes a deeper issue.

With most babies, you can take something away from them as long as you replace it with something equally interesting, and you won't usually get a big fuss. But toddlers are wise to that trick. They know what they want and they know how much they want it. They're also impulsive, and they haven't learned to think things through before acting (most adults, of course, haven't learned this very well either). Babies are impulsive too, but they don't have a very large sphere of influence. Toddlers, though, can grab just about anything away from just about anyone, and they certainly will try. And the same toddlers will impulsively shove or smack someone who takes something away from them. It's the original double standard: What's mine is mine and what's yours is mine too.

This impulsivity and lack of empathy explain why many toddlers are genuinely surprised when they grab a toy or shove another toddler and the other child bursts into tears. Slowly (way too slowly for most parents) children develop a dawning awareness that other people have needs and feelings too. Apparently those other kids aren't just props in a universe of that one supreme being, me.

In the meantime, you should certainly encourage your toddler to share and help him to understand the other child's point of view. You should listen empathically when he wants something terribly that he just can't have right now. You have a role to play, but it's important to realize that the real lessons about the value of sharing come from other children. Children teach sharing in rather ungentle ways—by grabbing a toy back, by screaming for Mom to intervene, by storming off and ending a perfectly fun game. Tough methods, perhaps, but usually effective. And as children begin to care how other people feel, and especially as they begin to care about playing with a peer, sharing becomes important to them—not just to Mom and Dad. Most toddlers figure out that while being bossy and possessive may get you all the toys, it also makes you lose out on those beginning steps of mutual friendship.

Children teach each other to share, but it takes longer than we want it to take. So our job is to gently underscore the lessons they learn from other children, not to lecture them or try to drag them kicking and screaming into stages of moral development they aren't ready for. We can say, "I don't think she liked that," "I don't think he likes this game as much as you do," "Looks to me like you're having trouble sharing and he's having trouble waiting," "I wonder if he yelled at you because you grabbed his truck," and so on.

You'll notice that those are pretty gentle reminders of the importance of sharing and the effects of not sharing. But this kind of "empathy coaching" is more effective than jumping in and saying, "Okay, ten minutes each, I'm setting a timer." That kind of solution, imposed by an adult, often leaves both children feeling miserable and the adult frustrated. Children often seem to prefer to keep fighting rather than follow this useful and rational suggestion about the timer. Compromising is way over their heads, and waiting for a timer to beep is too great a challenge for most toddlers. More importantly, those adult-imposed solutions interfere with children working things out on their own. Of course, if a bigger child always bosses around a littler one and hogs all the toys, you have to intervene in the name of basic fairness. But watch the whole scene before rushing to the rescue. The smaller child may have some subtle ways of her own to level the playing field.

You asked about toddlers sharing. My answer would have been a bit different if it were an older child who had difficulty with sharing or taking turns. This behavior, if it is extreme and if it continues, can indeed cost a child in the friendship department. Some children may need some remedial lessons in cause and effect (act too greedy and you'll lose friends), empathy (that really hurt her feelings), or fairness (you like to play with his toys at his house, so it's only fair to let him play with your toys here). Offer supervision, attention, encouragement, comfort, and a variety of toys, so that the children have a good foundation for working out the sharing struggles on their own.

Some children need some more attention to deeper issues of attachment and dependence and loss. Children whose emotional cups are empty, who feel unloved or lonely or fearful, may cling to their toys like lifelines and feel very threatened or anxious if anyone comes near them. These children need more than lessons in how to share. They need concentrated help in overcoming those deeper feelings. That might mean some playful parenting, such as grabbing a toy two kids are fighting over and running out the room so that they laughingly gang up on you. Or it might mean a period of increased love and attention to help ease the child's fears and clinginess.

But for a typical toddler, who wants what she wants right when she wants it, don't sweat it. Somehow, most of us step out of our self-centered universe in time to forge solid friendships.

Friendship Skills for Life

Q1: *My daughter is heading off to kindergarten in a few months. What can I do to ensure that she makes friends?*

Q2: *My daughter is about to start college, and I am worried about her making friends, because she is very shy. Is there anything I can do to help her?*

A: I just had to put these two questions together, because it is so striking that a parent of a five-year-old and a parent of an eighteen-year-old have exactly the same worry. And my answer is basically the same for both of them: Don't worry too much about it, because you've already done most of what you need to do.

In fact, I would bet that both of these children will stop crying before their moms do. Most children make a friend, or several friends, when they start kindergarten. And most make friends when they go off to college. Even shy children. In fact, shyness isn't as big a factor in friendship as many people think. The really important factor is early attachment.

Attachment is the word psychologists use to describe that process of filling up a child's empty cup by giving them love, food, comfort, and nurturing. The parent or primary caregiver can also be compared to a home base, a place for the child to start from and return to in between explorations. From the infant's point of view, attachment comes from being soothed when she is upset and from lively play when she is happy. From the adult's point of view, attachment is a matter of responding to the child's needs, mirroring the child's facial expressions and emotions, and falling in love with this incredible new human being.

When an infant's cup is kept full, refilled consistently whenever it is emptied by hunger, tiredness, loneliness, or being hurt, then the attachment is a secure one. If the adult caregiver is a secure home base, then the attachment is a sturdy one. Of course, not all attachments are this idyllic. Every child experiences frustration and loss. No parent can be perfectly responsive or consistent. As we shall see below, some attachments are marked more by anxiety or conflict. But if the attachment has gone fairly well, all the basics are there for later friendship development.

In fact, just as good friendships are the best predictor of adult happiness, good attachment is the best predictor of good peer relationships. So how does good attachment actually work its magic? Think about the groundwork you laid by snuggling close with your infant. Think of the ways you encouraged your toddler to explore the world, including the social world of other people. Think about the count-less times you comforted, dried tears, kissed skinned knees. The times you knew what your child needed and knew how to provide it. The warm gazing into each other's eyes. The reconciliations after a fuss or a blow-up. And the times you clapped and cheered at each new accomplishment. Listed below are the basic skills required for friendship. These skills do not appear full-blown out of nowhere. They are built up slowly through parenting and caregiving.

The essential friendship skills are:

- The enjoyment of the company of others
- A capacity for reciprocity, turn taking, cooperation and sharing
- Empathy
- Realistic, generally positive expectations that allow you to approach the world with confidence
- Problem-solving ability
- The ability to regulate aggressive impulses and other emotions
- The ability to read emotions, especially subtle and mixed emotions
- The ability to tolerate frustration
- The ability to "hold others in mind"
- Trust that others can and will hold you in mind
- Self-disclosure—the willingness and ability to show vulnerability

A quick look at this list reveals the close connection between friendship and early attachment. Children first learn to enjoy the company of others when they are infants, and an adult is content to just join the baby in endless staring into each other's eyes, and later in fun games of peekaboo and making funny faces. And the first turn-taking games happen in infancy too—taking turns smiling, for example. Parents discover that their baby isn't just a lump but is able to interact. And babies discover that they aren't just an extension of their mom but a separate being.

The ability to share and to handle frustration are tough lessons children learn in early childhood, as babies have to wait to be fed and have to compete for Mom's attention with siblings or Dad or work or sleep. Children learn empathy, of course, by a parent being empathic with them. And they learn how to read emotions by having a parent who is sensitive to the infant's emotions, and open with their own. This kind of sensitivity also helps children regulate and manage their emotions. That means that as they develop friendships they can handle and resolve conflict, find creative solutions to problems, and not be swamped by anger or envy when a friend wins a game or gets a new toy.

When a child's parenting and early attachment are consistent, the child develops realistic and generally positive expectations for the future. That's a big help in friendships, because if you always expect betrayal or rejection, you will usually get it. Consistency and emotional responsiveness also help children discern who is likely to be a good friend and whom they'd be better off avoiding.

The two items on that list that may be least familiar to you are the ability to "hold others in mind" and the trust that others can hold you in mind. This means that we think about our friends when they aren't around and that we believe they think about us. Dolly Madison said that friends halve our grief and double our joy, and this idea of holding in mind is how that friendship magic works. If something bad happens, we think immediately about telling our friend, and we know they will comfort us or make us laugh about it. If something good happens, we immediately think about telling our friend, to share it with them and experience the joy more fully. The simple eloquence of the phrase "I missed you" really means "I kept you in mind. Did you keep me in mind?"

Holding in mind means not just thinking about each other but thinking well about each other. That kind of openness to giving and receiving friendship comes directly from all those games of peekaboo (where Mom or Dad disappears and then comes right back) and hide-and-seek (where the suspense lasts a little longer) and all those times when someone actually showed up to pick the child up at day care or came in to comfort the child after a nightmare in the middle of the night.

In short, the basic requirement children need to maintain friendships—the belief that they are okay and that their friend is okay—is an outgrowth of all that early attachment. It springs directly from the confidence we try to give to babies that they are good and they are in good hands.

But what about the children who didn't have good early attachment? Some children are anxious and clingy in their attachment; others are withdrawn and shut down, or angry and resentful. Some children are difficult to attach to because they resist physical or emotional contact. The good news is that each new setting—whether it is kindergarten, chess club, townwide soccer team, high school, summer camp, or college—can provide another chance for a child to make up for deficits in early attachment. Sometimes it takes another child who also struggles with attachment or friendship. The two children can find a soul mate in each other and provide the closeness that eluded each of them before.

Are there lonely children in kindergarten and in college? Yes, there are. Not everyone makes a friend right away, though most make one or two or a bunch of friends eventually. Children who have already experienced a significant loss may face the most difficulty in making new friends, since they may hold back from connections in order to avoid another painful loss. So loneliness can breed more loneliness, until the seeds of a friendship bear fruit.

At times, if experiences or dynamics in the family have interfered with secure attachment, family therapy or play therapy may be needed. In other words, if you look at this list and see that your child doesn't have a good grasp of some of these skills, they aren't something he or she can learn from a book or a course. These skills are learned through interactions, through relationships. If they weren't instilled by early attachment, they need to be developed in new connections that the child finds safe and meaningful. That might be with you—perhaps you had trouble bonding with your child early on because of a loss, illness, or trauma in your own life, but you still have a chance to catch up and form a good attachment now. Or the attachment might be with an aunt or uncle who takes the child under a protective and loving wing, or a therapist or a teacher. Friendship skills are built through thousands upon thousands of tiny interactions between a child and a trusted adult, and later between the child and his or her peers.

The mom who's thinking about her college-bound student is worried about her daughter's shyness interfering with her making friends. But if we think about all of those friendship skills listed above, we can see that shyness really isn't that major a factor. Shyness is relevant only to overcoming the initial hurdles to knowing someone well enough for those skills to kick in. In other words, friendship takes practice. So listen empathically to shy children, but also give them gentle pushes to challenge their fears and try new things. If they resist, you may need to give bigger pushes, but you will then need to be available to listen to them cry or storm around about how hard it is, or how impossible it is, or how painful it is. As a formerly shy person who now does a lot of public speaking, I believe strongly that it is important to push oneself through this, and it helps to have someone cheering you on.

With all that said, there are still some things you can do to encourage and support your child's friendships in their new settings in kindergarten and college. It helps children (and grown-ups) a lot if they know someone before they walk in the door. So during the summer get a class list and make some phone calls to set up some play dates for the five-year-old. Get a list of freshmen from your neighborhood or your town and have them over for tea (or a game of basketball) for your college freshman. With your kindergartner, play games where the dolls or stuffed animals go to school, and follow your child's lead in this fantasy play. She may want you to be a really nice teacher or a really mean one, or she might want to play the role of the teacher herself. With a shy college-bound child, you can role-play meeting people and making small talk.

Once school or college has started, you still have an important role, but it is different from what you might think. Though you will arrange play dates for your kindergartner, you aren't in charge of seeing to it that she makes a friend or micromanaging her social life. And of course your college freshman needs to run her own social life. Your job is to be a home base, continuing that slow, patient, ongoing work of secure attachment. That means listening if your five-year-old comes home crying or if your eighteen-year-old calls home every few hours. (I always want to get together the parents who complain that their college-age children never call with the parents who complain that their child calls three or four times a day.) Make your home a place your children want to bring their friends to, the same way you made yourself a place your baby could come home to.

Have Faith in Development

Q: *Our four-and-a-half-year-old son is highly intelligent but lacks social intelligence. He'd rather play by himself, yet wonders why some other boys don't like him. We've set up play dates with one other child, and with some prompting he plays very well with him. However, if two children are visiting, our son prefers to do his own thing. Should we encourage our son to be more social? Is social skills training appropriate for a child his age? What should we look for in a social skills group?*

A: At what age *should* a child be able to play with other children in a group? At what age *should* children prefer the company of other children to that of adults? At what age *should* a child be able to cooperate with more than one person at a time? The answer to these questions is so complex that I must resort to humor. The boy you describe reminds me of a group I know. They are very bright, like to do their own thing, are often ill at ease socially, and don't react well in group settings. The people I'm thinking of is a group of Harvard professors. And the setting is faculty meetings.

If you think about it, the son you have described resembles some adults you already know. There are people in the workplace who don't congregate at the coffeemaker; there are people who prefer to work alone or perhaps problem-solve with only one other person. Some moms in your neighborhood socialize with almost everyone. Other folks stick close to their spouse. People connect with each other in an almost infinite variety of ways and have a tremendous variety of social styles. By the time they are adults we accept that people are the way they are.

The problem with a four-and-a-half-year-old, of course, is that we don't know yet how he is going to turn out. And no one can convince us that he is going to be fine. So we keep checking about every worrisome sign, frightened that he won't grow out of it, whatever "it" is. We want our children to master every social style. We want them to be brilliant and average, talkative and quiet, able to make one intense friendship *and* be at ease in a group.

Recently a reporter from a parenting magazine asked me if I would make a pie chart specifying how much a child should play alone, how much with parents, how much with siblings, and how much with peers. I politely refused. Watch your own child, I suggested, and help him have plenty of the kinds of play he likes best. And also give him gentle pushes once in a while to try something new.

Your son already has a preference for one kind of interaction—playing on his own—but he also complains that other kids don't like him. This has made you feel that there is something wrong with your son's social behavior. You may be worrying that he won't develop any further without a form of therapeutic intervention. I respectfully disagree with both of your conclusions. Let me address it as a philosophical matter and then concretely.

The kind of social creature your son is going to be at four and a half, at eight, or at twelve depends on three forces: his temperament, his rate of development, and his experience. Human beings are born with a certain kind of temperament. Both research and common sense tell us that some children come into the world as shy people and stay that way, while others are born confident. In families you often see one highly social child and another sibling who is more reserved. That is natural and inevitable.

Having more than one child makes it easier to see this. It is harder for parents to accept the inevitability of temperament when they have only one child. I'm imagining that the four-and-a-half-year-old boy you have described to me is an only child. And I'm also imagining that, temperamentally, he is a bit on the reserved side. We know from your description that when there is more than one child around, he prefers to play by himself. Two boys are too noisy and chaotic for him, or else he misses the control he experiences when he is with one child. (That could be one reason that he says other kids don't like him. They may reject his attempts to always be in charge of the game.) That's temperament. We know that because when we compare him to other boys his age we find boys who seem to love being in a big group—and both types of boys are healthy.

Now, what about his rate of development? Just because he prefers one friend, is he always going to be this way? He might, but it is equally likely that he will change. Have you ever heard someone say, "I used to be so shy when I was younger"? People often tell you that they "outgrew" some striking aspect of their childhood selves. And they did change over time. We all did—and at very different rates. That is what development is about: growing and developing a broader repertoire in all areas of life. Social skills are skills, like riding a bike. It takes time to develop them.

Finally, there is life experience. Again common sense tells us that being one of five children from a highly social family connected to a large church community is likely to make a child more comfortable with groups than if he were the only child of quiet, reserved parents who spent a great deal of time at home. We have an impact by shaping the kinds of social experiences our children have. And you are doing that for your son. You arrange play dates, you do some prompting to help him know how to play with his friends. By your report, this is successful. He has had some social failures, but he is learning and growing. Those words are music to the ears of a child psychologist.

It is for that reason that I do not want you to look for a social skills group for him. He does not have a problem yet that he cannot outgrow through a combination of development and life experience. I don't think you should treat him as if he were defective or a failure. He is too young for that. He is growing at his own rate, he has his own comfort zone, and—perhaps most importantly—most of childhood *is* social skills training. That's what children do for each other naturally as they play together. Kids teach each other how to get along with other children.

Children who attend preschool are more socially competent earlier than children who do not. Is your son in preschool? If not, he might simply not have had enough social experiences yet to make him feel socially confident. But he will begin to hone those skills as soon as he enters kindergarten.

Are you worried that he is not going to be socially capable in kindergarten and needs preparation to be successful there? I assure you that he will encounter a variety of social styles in kindergarten and will be able to learn what he needs to learn to be okay with his classmates. Put more faith in development! It is an unstoppable force, and school is, in itself, a powerful social skills group. To paraphrase a famous book title, he's going to learn most of what he needs to know in kindergarten.

Addressing a Social Skills Deficit

Q: *During several conferences and meetings at my son's school I have been told that he has a "social skills deficit." But even after a lot of discussion, I'm not sure exactly what that means. Can you explain the social skills that kids need to get along with their peers?*

A: Let's imagine two first graders, Sarah and David, who are in the same classroom. During free-choice time after lunch one day, David walks up to two other children who are putting together a city out of blocks. He watches them for a while and then says, "That's really cool. What is it?" One of the other children explains that it's a parking garage. David says, "I'll go get some cars," and runs off to the toy shelf. He comes back with a handful of cars and asks the other two kids which ones should go in the garage. They all concentrate on deciding which cars should go where. Another child walks over and "accidentally" knocks over part of the block city. David says, "Hey, you knocked over our tower! Help us build it back up again." He notices that the boy who built that part of the tower is very upset, and goes over to sit next to him. "We'll build it back up even better, okay?"

Meanwhile Sarah has gone over to another group of kids, who are drawing. "What is that supposed to be?" she asks one in an accusatory tone. "It doesn't look like anything!" The other child turns her back on Sarah. "I want to draw too!" she shouts, grabbing for some of the pencils next to one of the children. "I'm using those!" says the other child firmly, putting her hand protectively over the pile. Sarah runs to the teacher and bursts into tears, saying that the other kids are not letting her play.

If we look at the difference between these two scenarios—each of which is played out over and over in every school, every day—we can see the essential elements of social competence, or social skills: *emotional regulation, turn taking, joining a group, giving positive attention to others, sociability, social knowledge, tuning in to social cues, and balancing autonomy with relationships.*

Emotional regulation is like having a dimmer switch on our feelings instead of just an on-off button. The ability to tolerate frustration and manage other strong emotions is one of the most basic prerequisites for good peer relations. We simply can't reap the benefits of companionship unless we are able to handle our emotions, at least a bit. When someone knocks over the block tower, David takes it in stride. He is probably upset, but it doesn't overwhelm him. When Sarah hits a roadblock in her goal of joining the group at the drawing table, she falls apart. With healthy emotional regulation, we can feel anger, jealousy, or excitement and channel that emotion effectively, instead of being overloaded with feeling. David can soothe himself and can even soothe his classmate, who he sees is more upset than he is. Sarah can't soothe herself and goes to the teacher for comfort—but she isn't even aware of wanting comfort. Instead she asks the teacher for justice, wanting an adult to overturn the verdict of the "lower court" of Sarah's peers. With her difficulty in emotional regulation, we might expect Sarah to be upset about this all day, which will manifest itself in irritability and anger, or perhaps frequent "accidents" that she can use as a pretext to cry or have a tantrum.

Taking turns is an obvious skill, essential for playing well with others. Again, tolerating frustration is part of the program. For some children the key issue isn't frustration but simply the idea of turns. David understands that there is a rhythm to play, even if it isn't a board game or sports activity with specific turns. On the other hand, Sarah plows into the drawing activity, oblivious to the need to take turns with the colored pencils.

Joining a group is a skill that school counselors or therapists spend a great deal of time on when they teach a course in social skills training. David is a great model for group entry. He comes in slowly, sizes up the scene, says something related to the play, and eases himself in. He sets up a situation where the other children are not threatened. They don't have to worry that he will take over or ruin their game. Sarah, in contrast, is unskilled in this area. She tumbles in headlong without checking out the situation first. She attempts to grab some playthings that the other kids are in the middle of using, which sets up an immediate conflict. She insults one of the people in the group she wants to enter, hoping perhaps that this will give her status. Instead it makes the group defensive, and so they circle their wagons, leaving her on the outside.

David gave positive attention to others when he started his approach with a compliment. Sarah began with an insult. Children with good social skills have a great knack for giving sincere appreciation that doesn't come across as manipulative flattery. That's because their goal is to engage, to play together, to build friendship as they build block towers. Children who lack this skill also want to make friends and play together, but they are stuck. They get sidetracked into the goal of getting their way, being in control, or asserting their own superiority.

Sociability is one of those things that is hard to define but easy to see when it's there or when it's missing. Sociability includes a generally upbeat outlook on life, a genuine interest in others, an expectation of fairness and equity, and, above all, emotional warmth. Even these brief vignettes make it clear that David has a high level of this quality of sociability and Sarah lacks it.

In order to succeed socially, we need social knowledge. Children pick this up just from living in a family and living in a society, though some pick it up better than others. Social knowledge means having a pretty good idea about what's going to happen if you grab another child's toy or if you offer him a turn with a special toy of yours. It means knowing the norms and customs of your subculture—in this case, the subculture of the American first-grade classroom. It means knowing that when one child says, "I'm the red Power Ranger!" an appropriate response is "I'm the white Power Ranger!" not "What's a Power Ranger?" David knew that cars belong in garages and that lots of boys like cars, so he made a pretty safe bet that he could be included in the game if he brought over some toy cars. Sarah did not understand the dynamics of the drawing table—everyone sits quietly, shares the colored pencils without conflict, and compliments each other's drawings. And she compounded her error by going to the teacher to tattle. She apparently hasn't figured out yet that this is a sure way to be ostracized by the group.

But knowing the social ins and outs is irrelevant if a child does not tune in to social cues. Sarah missed the significance of the other girl turning her back on her, while David tuned in to the pauses of the conversation in order to interject his idea at just the right moment. He also tuned in to the emotions of the boy whose tower was knocked down.

Like a block tower, friendship is a balancing act. It involves careful readjustment between autonomy and relationship. David wants to play with cars, but he also wants to play with other boys in his class, who are playing blocks. If he insists on playing with cars, he may end up playing alone. If he joins the block game, he has given up on his own desires. In this case, he found a perfect balance. It isn't always so easy, and sometimes you have to give up one or the other temporarily and trust that it will balance out in the end. Sarah can't seem to find a way to achieve this balance at all. She wants desperately to be part of the group, and she wants desperately to be the only one with a good drawing. She can't figure out how to have both.

Why do some children (and adults) have deficits in some or all of these social skills? Sometimes the difficulties are hardwired—there may be a neurological reason that a child has trouble regulating emotions or paying attention to social details. Other children lack these skills because they missed out on the important lessons of early attachment, which set the stage for all these aspects of social competence. Some have no chance for practice because their family is extremely isolated or because of frequent moves. (Of course, some children who move frequently develop exceptional social skills as a way of navigating the repeated demands of joining new groups and making new friends.)

Shyness is not the same thing as having a social skills deficit, but a shy child may not get as much practice with social situations as outgoing children do. Most shy children do a lot of watching and learning from the sidelines, though, and are able to put these skills into practice once they are ready to dive in (or tiptoe in) to the social seas. At the other extreme, impulsive children may experience rejection from peers who can't handle their intensity or their bull-in-a-china-shop approach. But on the other hand, extremely outgoing and demonstrative children get lots of chances for practice.

The best approach to social skills deficits is early

intervention—stepping in to provide some specific training and help in the areas outlined above, before negative feedback cycles and bad reputations develop. Many schools provide friendship groups or other types of informal social skills training in the early grades for children who especially need them. Other schools offer a more formal curriculum in social skills, which offers the basics to those kids who need them and provides more advanced social training, such as win-win strategies, for children who have the basics down.

When working on social skills with a child, it is important to remember that the key childhood skills are not exactly the same as adult social skills. For instance, children rarely introduce themselves to one another. They just start playing. They might ask another child's name but not think to offer their own name. Good peer social skills among children don't usually include saying please and thank you. Many parents confuse good manners with good social skills. Manners may be important, but the skills listed above are more crucial to social acceptance. Sometimes well-meaning parents tell their kids to simply walk up to other children and ask, "Can I play?" But I always teach children not to *ever* say that, because it's like an engraved invitation for another child to say no. The refusal comes not out of spite or meanness but from a lack of social skills of their own. Instead, suggest to children that they go stand nearby, make relevant contributions to the conversation, give positive attention, and offer assistance.

Embracing Imaginary Friends

Q: *My daughter has an imaginary friend. At first we thought this was cute, but it is really getting carried too far, and I'd like to get her to put this childish thing aside and be more involved with her real friends.*

A: I think imaginary friends are almost always a wonderful thing for a child, and nothing at all to worry about. But before I get into the benefits to children of imaginary friendships, let me address some of your specific concerns.

You don't say how old your child is, but I seldom, if ever, worry that an imaginary friendship has gone on for "too long." Imaginary friendships are most common between the ages of three and six, but I have seen perfectly healthy children of eight, ten, or twelve with imaginary friendships. I am biased, of course, because I had an imaginary friend in sixth grade. You might begin to worry if your child asks for another suitcase so his imaginary friend can go with him to college! But of course many older teenagers and even young adults—boys as well as girls—take stuffed animals and other substitute friends with them when they move away from home.

Your other worry is that this imaginary friendship will get in the way of your daughter's real friendships. Nothing could be further from the truth. It is much more accurate to think of imaginary friendships as steps along the way to real friendships. The transition might take longer than you would like, but the number one rule of child development is that it always goes at the child's pace, not the parent's pace. If that pace includes a pause to focus on an imaginary friend, so be it.

The deepest worry some parents have about a child's imaginary friends is that their child might be psychotic—out of touch with reality. I can assure you that if this is the case, you will see many other, more serious and obvious signs of mental illness. So don't be alarmed if your child seems to believe in the reality of her friend or if she insists that you treat the friend as a real member of the family. Even young children who are just learning about fantasy and reality know that they are playing make-believe. They are actually doing something that is mentally quite complex. They aren't just pretending to have a friend; they are pretending that they think this friend is real. They don't need to be clobbered over the head with the difference between fantasy and reality. At least 99 percent of the time these friendships are an expression of the child's creativity and imagination as well as being a step forward on the path from being totally self-centered to being a true friend.

With all that said, it can get annoying when a young child constantly says, "Don't sit there, you'll crush Nunny!" or "You forgot to set a place at the table for Albert the Aardvark." It's no wonder it's annoying. One of the purposes of this type of play is that it is a great way for children to exert their power over adults—a little gentle payback for the way we exert our power over them most of the time. In any event, there is no benefit to you or your child in getting into power struggles over imaginary friends, even when you think the child has taken this imaginary friendship too far. Either your child will win this struggle and you are back where you started, or you will win but your child will deeply resent your intrusion into this unusual but deeply meaningful relationship. If your child is getting whiny and obnoxious about this imaginary friend, and you are getting aggravated about having to kiss the friend goodnight and read it a bedtime story every evening, it will help to set aside a half hour or an hour to play this game cheerfully and enthusiastically. That special attention usually lets the child ease up a little on imposing the imaginary friend onto your family's life.

Why do children invent imaginary friends? The first and simplest purpose is for practice with friendship. Children don't just instantly know how to do things in life, especially big things such as making and keeping friends. They often use play to practice new skills, the same way that lion cubs practice wrestling and fighting with one another. Every child learns to help Mommy or Daddy dress him before he learns to fully dress himself. And children can do things in play that they can't do yet in the "real world." My favorite example of this is a boy who could not for the life of him sit still during circle time in kindergarten. He couldn't raise his hand and wait to be called on, and he couldn't let anyone else speak without interrupting. But when he was playing school, as a pretend dramatic game, he could do all those things perfectly.

So what does that have to do with imaginary friends? With Nunny or Fogger or Albert the Aardvark, you get to practice being a friend and having a friend. Think about the important transition from playing alone to playing with another child. It's fun to share play with someone, but it's hard, because you also have to share the decision making, share the toys, and share being first. Most children eventually decide that it's worth giving up some autonomy in exchange for camaraderie. But others need to think about that for a while longer, so they practice with an imaginary friend, or with their dolls and stuffed animals. With those friends they can be completely in charge of the play while pretending to cooperate and share. Even after a child is able to engage in mutual play, he or she can get exhausted from all that sharing and need a play place to be the boss, yet still not be totally alone. Imaginary friends can come in handy at times like that.

If we set aside the obvious limitation of imaginary friends—that they're not real—we can see the benefits of such a friend. They are always ready to play, and they happily go along with the child's proposals for what to play and how to play and who gets to be the red Power Ranger. Imaginary friends always share, never grab, and are always willing to take the blame for the spilled milk or broken lamp. No wonder so many of us find real friends a disappointment or such a pain in the neck sometimes!

Why do imaginary friends most often appear around age three or four? In a groundbreaking 1961 book about the life of preschoolers, *The Magic Years,* Selma Fraiberg goes back a year or two to describe the power of being a toddler: "The magician is seated in his high chair and looks upon the world with favor. He is at the height of his powers. If he closes his eyes, he causes the world to disappear. If he opens his eyes, he causes the world to come back. If there is harmony within him, the world is harmonious. If rage shatters his inner harmony, the unity of the world is shattered. If desire arises within him, he utters the magic syllables that cause the desired object to appear. His wishes, his thoughts, his gestures, his noises command the universe."

As a toddler develops into a preschooler, he or she can't remain master of the universe in the same way. Other children's needs must be taken into account unless the child chooses to be utterly alone. If you want to play dress-up and the other child wants to be the princess, you have to decide whether to insist on being the princess, risking the continuation of the game, or agree to be the lady-in-waiting this time. You can no longer just close your eyes and make it so. Sometimes you have to choose between connection and control.

This balance between connection and control is tough to achieve. We all struggle with it on a daily basis, even when we're all grown up. Let's say we want to go to a particular movie with a particular friend. That friend wants to do something different. Do we go to the movie alone or go to the other activity in order to be with the friend? How risky is it to deliver an ultimatum? What if the other person delivers an ultimatum first?

Of course, we don't usually invent an imaginary friend who will accompany us to the movie of our choice. I'm not sure if that's because we have grown up and can make that choice between control and connection more easily, or just because we lack imagination!

The great British psychoanalyst D. W. Winnicott coined the term "transitional object" to describe young children's security blankets and similar objects. These objects serve as a transition between the mother (or, as psychoanalysts would say, the mother's breast) and the outside world. With her blankie, a child can take the first steps of independence and still have her mother with her. The child gives an inanimate object a symbolic meaning as a stand-in for the mother or primary caretaker. The mother isn't always available, and the child hasn't yet figured out how to get all her needs met from the outside world. In the meantime, the blanket provides comfort and security.

Imaginary friends serve very much the same purposes, offering a transition to real friendship, a comfort in times of upset or loss, a way to have both connection and control. When children have overwhelming feelings or irresistible impulses, they may feel out of control. They may worry that they will lose their connection with their parents for having that feeling or doing that naughty thing. Enter the imaginary friend. Imaginary friends are great for projecting these unwanted feelings or impulses onto: "Nunny did it, not me!" "Fogger is scared—can you stay with him a little longer before you turn the light out?" "Albert the Aardvark was very naughty today and pinched the baby." These projections often annoy parents, who see them as evasions of responsibility. But from a psychological point of view they're not a big problem. Children are just using play to help themselves understand and manage their emotions and their impulses. Instead of getting hung up in the reality of who really pinched the baby or who is really scared, parents can use these moments as opportunities to set limits, to comfort, to support, and to teach children how to put their feelings and impulses into words and safe actions.

Some parents assume that an imaginary friend means that their child must be lonely. But this is not so. As I've said, most imaginary friendships are not a substitute for friends but a step toward having friends. But if children are rejected and lonely, the fantasy can provide emotional support and solace. As Doris Fromberg and Doris Bergen write in *Play from Birth to Twelve and Beyond*, their textbook on play,

"For the excluded child, imagination also is an important support system. It can transport the child to other times and places that may be happy, vengeful, or comforting." An unhappy child might even be mean to an imaginary friend, acting out what was done to him. More often, an unhappy child clings to the imaginary friendship, and if he is lucky, he will find a real friend who can provide the same amount of comfort along with the joys of true companionship. As a parent, you can help a child use the imaginary friendship to learn how to be a good friend.

Imaginary friends arrive in their own time, and they leave in their own time too. Most often they just fade away, but they can also become a focal point for expressing feelings that are bottled up inside a child. I had friends who moved across the country, and their oldest son, who was eleven at the time, acted as though he had no feelings of loss or sadness about leaving his home and school and friends, no feelings of trepidation about making new friends. But immediately after arriving in his new home he began to talk about having an imaginary puppy, which was his constant companion. A couple of weeks later, as he was settling into his new school and new neighborhood, that puppy "ran away," and the boy had a long, long cry. He used this imaginary friend first for comfort and then as an excuse to let out all those tears he had been holding in so bravely.

Popularity and Power

Q: *Is there such a thing as being too popular? My daughter is extremely popular, and she works hard at staying that way. I* *was never very popular as a girl, so this is new territory for me. I kind of enjoy seeing her so socially successful, but I also remember the mean things that the popular girls did to my friends and me. I don't want her to be like that!*

A: Your concern about the potential dangers of popularity makes me think of two famous quotes. One is from Yogi Berra, the baseball legend with a unique way with words. Talking about a popular nightspot, he said, "Nobody goes there anymore, it's too crowded." The other quote, from Lord Acton, is better known: "All power tends to corrupt, but absolute power corrupts absolutely." And there you have the two pitfalls of excess popularity. Popularity can make you mean, or it can leave you lonely.

Power corrupts. And power that comes merely from being popular tends to corrupt even more. In a relentless "cycle of popularity"—a term coined by sociologist Donna Eder—a very popular child often tumbles from his or her pedestal, sometimes falling all the way down to being the new social outcast. To paraphrase Yogi Berra, nobody likes her anymore because she's too popular.

These falls from grace are most likely to happen during middle school or early in high school. The class queen bee or alpha male might take a tumble as other people start to see her or him as stuck up. How does this happen? Children who are extremely popular get many more invitations for friendship and events than they can accept, and everyone they turn down has the potential to accumulate resentment. And a group of peers who are all turned down—or put down—can gang together to turn the tables. The more corrupt (or mean) a powerful figure is in his or her social power, the longer it may take to fall, because everyone else is intimidated. But when a cruel king or queen is deposed, he or she can fall very far indeed.

Eventually many of the most popular kids—especially girls—are dethroned by the same group who elevated them in the first place. The dethroning happens quicker if a powerful new leader emerges to challenge the queen or if a new girl comes into the class and changes the group dynamics. Once deposed, former queen bees are often subjected to cruel reprisals from former victims, and even from former loyal followers. These attacks are self-righteously justified as being "only what she deserves" for having been so mean to others when she ruled the roost. Even adults may condone this vengeance against a onetime queen, feeling that she does indeed deserve it as punishment for her earlier tyranny. Teachers who try to come to the aid of a deposed queen, now in exile, often find themselves alone in the staff lounge defending her while everyone else enjoys the spectacle of the reversal of fortunes.

In one school, two clique leaders had cemented their positions as co-queens in third grade. At the beginning of fourth grade, though, their dethroning was already under way. A group of girls had united in denouncing the two as stuck-up and mean. Meanwhile, another group still loyal to the clique vied with each other for attention and recognition from the leaders. A few other girls held themselves aloof, trying to maintain connections with both groups—but that became increasingly difficult. (When a fight for dominance occurs, children will often make their classmates choose sides: "If you're with her, you're against me.")

These two girls survived fourth grade as queens by

becoming more inclusive in their reign. They backed off from ruling with an iron fist and from trying to dominate everyone else's social experience—and the group allowed them to continue to be in charge.

Sometimes dethroning of the king and queen takes place when other children start to lose interest in the popularity wars. Eventually, even though they may have yearned for popularity, the other kids develop a healthy skepticism about group status. At the same time, they come to a greater appreciation of having a friend, someone loyal and reliable. That leaves the queen without a hive to rule.

One of our main goals as parents and educators has to be to support friendship—a much more lasting force in children's lives than popularity. If popularity is a cycle, then supporting friendship is equally important for those at the top as for those at the bottom. Take those at the top. If you ask young children what it means to be popular, they will say it means that you have the most friends. But if you ask middle-schoolers or high-schoolers, they will tell you that the most popular kids can never be sure if they have any friends at all or if people are just sucking up to them because of their position in the student hierarchy. As the importance of popularity starts to fade, children may say, "Oh yeah, she's still popular, but no one likes her." I think that means that a child can still wield social power but not be able to enjoy the support and sustenance of a warm and mutual friendship.

I mentioned that popular girls are more likely to take a tumble than popular boys are. That's because the whole issue of status and dominance is usually less emotional and less volatile for boys. However, boys who let their popularity go to their head (or are seen by others as letting it go to their head) can also take a fall. While they are at the top, they may have trouble with close friendships because everyone sees them only as the alpha males, not as regular boys who need friends. It is quite common for the most popular boy in a school to come to the school psychologist or guidance counselor saying he has no one to talk to. This isolation happens because to maintain his position he also has to maintain his cool pose. He is not able to reveal to any of the other boys that he has worries or troubles like theirs.

One more problem with popularity is that it is never a done deal. Maintaining status is a constant struggle. The pressure to set the standards of attractiveness, status, and attention from the opposite sex can interfere with a popular child's ability to maintain good friendships—and with his school achievement. Moreover, when the child falls in the inevitable cycle, the pain of that fall can lead to further difficulties with friendships and academics.

You say that you are glad your child is a social success, but you worry about the pitfalls of too much popularity. The problem, as I have suggested, isn't really too much popularity, but too much emphasis on popularity as the be-all and end-all of social success. Take a broader view, one that includes good friendships, good leadership skills, kindness, and inclusion. That's the kind of social success that is not susceptible to a cycle of flying too high and crashing too low.

A Perspective on Pain

Q: *I'm terribly worried about what will happen to my daughter when she heads to middle school next year. I had a hideous* *experience in middle school, and I can't bear to think of her going through even a fraction of what happened to me.*

A: I have some bad news and some good news for you. And as a special treat, I have some *really* good news for you. The bad news is that your daughter will experience some emotional pain in middle school. Almost every child does. (I would say every single child does, but I suppose it's possible that someone somewhere breezes through without a social care in the world. I haven't met that person yet.) Some of your daughter's pain will seem unbearable at the time it is happening—but she will bear it. And so will you. That's the good news. She will most likely get through her painful experiences, as the great majority of children do, and as you did. Yes, you still remember the pain of that time, but it didn't destroy your life. It may even have made you a more empathic parent and friend.

The really good news comes from a study by Martha Putallaz and her colleagues at Duke University. The study is described in the book *Learning About Relationships,* edited by Steve Duck. Putallaz asked mothers of preschoolers about their own childhoods, and she discovered that the mothers formed three separate groups. One group had warm, positive memories of their relations with their peers. These mothers remembered themselves as being socially competent children and considered themselves nurturing mothers. They also viewed their own children as socially competent. These are the lucky parents and children, the ones who face a child's middle-school years with sunny confidence. They know that a bad day or a bad spell is a bump in an otherwise predictable and positive road. By contrast, the other two groups of mothers recalled predominantly negative peer experiences. One group remembered themselves as having been socially incompetent children, and they saw their own children as being socially incompetent also. This group of mothers viewed themselves as not being especially nurturing, and they were quite anxious about their children's social development. Unfortunately, they were unable to transform that anxiety into effective help for their children. (Parents who see themselves in this description might consider individual psychotherapy as a way of recovering from the lasting effects of painful early experiences so that they can become more nurturing and supportive with their own children. At a minimum, parents who don't feel they know how to be nurturing can benefit greatly from parenting classes and talking openly with other parents about their own childhoods and their worries and hopes for their children.)

The third group is the most interesting, and I'm guessing it is the group you would belong to if you had been a subject in this study. Like the second group of mothers, this group reported mostly anxious and lonely childhood peer experiences, and they remembered themselves as having been socially incompetent children. However, they described themselves as nurturing mothers. Of the three groups, these mothers made the most effective efforts to intervene on behalf of their children's peer relations. The mothers themselves were not sure whether or not their children were socially competent. But peers, teachers, and independent observers all rated their children as highly socially competent. Why is this such good news? It shows that horrible social experiences are not inevitably passed on to the next generation. A mom who had a bad time socially herself can't help but be anxious for her daughter or son, but if she channels that anxiety into nurturing and support, things go well for the child socially. A nurturing mother supports her child and her child's friendships.

Martha Putallaz and her colleagues make a very important observation about the three different groups of mothers that they studied. The mothers in the third group, who had a painful childhood socially but were determined to have it be different for their own children, were best able to coach their children to be good friends and to have good friends. The other two groups felt they lived in a world that was either benevolent or malevolent and so saw children as either lucky or doomed. A parent in the first group might ignore or minimize her child's true suffering, because she sees the world as sunny and bright. A parent in the second group might expect the worst and fail to notice that her child is actually doing fine. But the mothers in the third group—who lived through hell and came out on top—are able to tune in to what their children are really experiencing and what they really need.

Another piece of good news is that sometimes it does not even take a whole generation for a pattern of social cruelty or rejection to be changed. Many individual children break this cycle all on their own. They make a conscious decision to be kind to others even though they were treated badly themselves. A friend told me that her experience of third grade was so brutal that her parents had to transfer her to a new school, where things improved. But the experience of social pain led this child to make a decision to commit herself to kindness. She vowed *never* to tease or ostracize another child. And she never did.

When the Group Causes Trouble

Q: *I am perfectly comfortable leaving my fourteen-year-old at home alone for a few hours. But I would never leave two or three (or more) fourteen-year-olds in the house alone. Why do kids seem to get in so much more trouble when they're in a group?*

A: You're right to be nervous about turning your house over to a group of fourteen-year-olds. They will almost always get into more trouble together than alone. Psychologists call this the "risky shift," and it means that a group of people makes riskier decisions together than most of them would make as individuals.

Here's how it works: Imagine that ten people are each given a hundred dollars and are asked separately how much of it they want to bet on a single flip of a coin. Most likely a couple of people will bet it all, a couple more will bet very little or none of it, and most will bet a modest amount. But if you put the same ten people together, give them a thousand dollars to share, and tell them they have to decide together how much of it to bet on a coin toss, they are likely to risk most of it. The group as a whole almost always makes a riskier decision than the average individual's decision.

Groups are also susceptible to a process called groupthink, in which individual members are reluctant to criticize a plan once it is proposed, no matter how many misgivings they may have about the plan privately. Since the plan is likely to be a risky one because of the risky shift, these two group dynamics can add up to some unwise decisions—especially if you happen to be fourteen.

For some teenagers who are extreme risk takers anyway, there isn't much of a difference between being in a group or alone. They are going to make risky decisions no matter what. But for the majority, the group's decision will be a little riskier—or much riskier—than what they would have decided on their own.

Fourteen-year-olds aren't making decisions about betting their money, of course. They're interested in whether to follow the rules, stretch the rules, break the rules—or creatively come up with new ideas that aren't even covered by the rules.

Let's take a closer look at how the risky shift and groupthink cast their spell. First of all, people feel stronger in a group. They may even think they are invincible or invulnerable. That feeling can be very helpful for a football team that has a strong sense of group identity, but it can also lead to extreme decisions with little or no thought for the consequences. Besides, there is the illusion that there will be no individual consequences of a bad decision, because it is a group decision. If things go wrong, each person in the group thinks, "It won't be *my* fault and it won't be on *my* head."

Teenagers vary quite a bit in terms of their impulsivity—their natural inclination to take risks. So when you say that you are comfortable leaving your teenager home alone, I assume that's because he or she has a low or moderate level of risk taking. But gather a group or even a pair of teenagers, and one is likely to be more of a risk taker than the others. Teenagers tend to value risk taking highly, so the more daring person's ideas and opinions will be given greater weight than the thoughtful, careful, cautious opinions of the kids who are averse to risk. Groupthink enters the picture once the risk taker has spoken, making it hard for anyone else to speak up without sounding like a goody-goody. The voice of reason remains silent.

On his or her own, away from the influence of the risky shift or groupthink, your child uses an inner moral compass. Everyone has one of these handy gadgets and uses it as a guide through the maze of deciding what's right and what's wrong—though some people don't consult theirs very often or very carefully. A moral compass also shows the child a preview of how his or her parents will react, and other possible consequences of behavior. But the risky shift replaces that individual moral compass with a group's moral compass. When a group decides something together, it automatically feels like a moral decision, because the whole group agreed to it. But in fact it wasn't really agreed to by anyone in the group, not in the sense of each person weighing the decision against his or her own inner moral compass.

We all know that groups can go terribly astray in terms of their moral reasoning. Everyone not in the group can easily be considered an outsider, a legitimate target, a nonhuman. This is, of course, the foundation for hate crimes and genocide. But on a smaller scale, it affects every group, because we're all prone to that feeling of us versus them and the idea that if you're not with us you're against us. Speaking out against a risky, immoral, or illegal decision is hard to do because that makes you an outsider yourself.

The views of a "good kid" who consults his moral compass are often overlooked in a risky shift. An enthusiastic tide of opinion railroads quiet opposition, and it looks like everyone has agreed. As the tide rolls on, any last-minute protests are dismissed or the protesters are pressured to conform to the group's decision.

So besides providing more supervision and getting a better lock for the liquor cabinet, what can we do to help protect teenagers from the negative effects of risky shift and groupthink? It helps to explain to them the power of group dynamics and talk about group decisions in those terms. It helps to say, "I trust you and your friends individually, but I know that dumb decisions get made sometimes by smart people when they get together in groups. How are you all going to make sure that doesn't happen?" You can also role-play different scenarios with your children: "If you guys are home alone and someone says, 'Let's take your dad's car,' what are you going to say?" For teenagers, some risk taking is inevitable. Programs such as Outward Bound or the National Outdoor Leadership School offer wonderful opportunities for safe but exciting risk taking, and for learning about effective group decision making.

Finally, it's important to remember that the risky shift is not *always* bad. Sometimes the support of a group can make for boldness, not anarchy. A child who is too timid to enter the science fair, try out for the school play, or join the school orchestra can benefit when a couple of friends join in and they all take the risk of trying something new together.

A Matter of Style

Q: *My son, who never cared the tiniest bit what he wore or how he looked, has suddenly become a clotheshorse. He insists*

*on trips to the mall, of all places, something he wouldn't have
dreamed of doing just a few months ago. I used to have to beg
him to buy new clothes to replace the ragged ones, and to comb
his hair. Now he uses gel, for goodness' sake. What's going on?*

A: To answer you I consulted an expert, my sixth-grade
daughter. Emma laughed when I read this question out loud.
This was no mystery to her. She guessed that your son is a
sixth grader, though he could be in fifth or seventh, depending on the school. I'd have to agree with her guess. Emma
told me a story about a boy in her class that I think will shed
some light on the stranger in your house who looks vaguely
liked a cleaned up version of your son.

"In fourth grade," Emma said, "it didn't really matter
how you acted, like if something was a 'boy thing' or a 'girl
thing.' There was a kid and he always used to sit with his legs
crossed, and that was fine in fourth grade. At some point
during fifth grade, though, everybody—I mean all the boys,
including him—stopped sitting that way. I don't think it was
ever a rule or anything, but it just wasn't the thing to do. But
now, in sixth grade, there's a boy who is new to the school.
And he sits like that. Except now it's 'wrong.' "

I asked her what she meant that it was wrong, and she
explained that boys just didn't sit that way. I asked her why
not—what was the big deal?

"I know that *I* don't care how he sits," she insisted, "and
I'm sure if I asked my friends privately, *they* wouldn't care
how he sits, but in a group . . ."

Emma trailed off, as though the rest were obvious. But I
asked her what she meant by it being different in a group.

"Well," she went on, "in a group the boy-girl thing is

stronger, and it's just wrong, or as kids would say, 'It's not right.' And the sad thing is that he doesn't even know it."

So even though each individual child would insist that it doesn't matter how you sit, somehow the group as a whole has a different opinion. And being new to the school is clearly no excuse for not knowing the rules.

I jumped in again at this point in Emma's story because I was surprised to hear that this boy was being excluded from coolness because he sat in a supposedly "girly" way. He is tall and athletic and seems to my untrained (that is, old) eye to be both cool and masculine.

Emma set me straight. "I wouldn't say it, but as my friends would say it, he has no sense of style. He can't dress. I guess his friends don't really tell him that the goal in sixth grade is to get girls to like you and to look nice, because he's their friend, and maybe they don't want to hurt his feelings. And if a girl tells him, he doesn't take it seriously, because what does he care what a girl thinks? But that's because he doesn't get it that the main priority in sixth grade is to get a girl to like you. The boys may act like they don't care, but they all put gel in their hair and are with the style. Even the most unpopular boys are with the style—even Andrew is with the style—but this boy is not."

Now I was really surprised, because when she said "even Andrew" I knew what she meant. Andrew is the boy in her grade whom I would have voted least likely to be "with the style." But in fact, like your son, Andrew got a clue and snapped into action—gelling his hair, wearing the right clothes, and trawling for a "girlfriend" (Emma refers to boyfriend-girlfriend behavior at this age as "virtual going out," since it's all a matter of *talking* about who likes whom, with no actual dating or even talking on the phone. All the talking is with other members of your own gender about the romantic process, rather than actually engaging in much romance.)

In your son's case, and for the majority of teenagers, the demands of the group are fairly benign. They're able and willing to get with the program. In fact, they don't experience themselves as being pressured or coerced into a cult of masculinity or femininity. They experience it as a choice. It's a new stage in their lives, to be relished even if it has bittersweet, or bitter, moments.

But for some kids, the pressure to be someone they aren't can be brutal. Children who are gay or lesbian, for example, or who just don't fit the stereotypical gender norms often have to choose between pretending to follow the rules about boy-girl behavior or being targeted if they don't. A terrible choice, if it even is a choice. Either result—being untrue to oneself or being rejected by the group—can be devastating. And some children sacrifice their integrity by conforming to the group and are ostracized anyway, a double whammy.

On a brighter note, your son clearly *has* a clue. And he isn't really a stranger someone substituted for your scruffy boy. I know it's a shock to parents that something your child would never do happily out of love or loyalty or obedience to you—dress well and smell nice—is something he or she will do slavishly if it's demanded by the group, or blissfully for someone he or she has a crush on. It may be a shock for you, but your son is right on schedule, whether you're ready or not.

When a Boy Falls Head over Heels

Q: *My teenage son has his first girlfriend, and he seems to be head over heels in love with her. That's all fine, but he has stopped hanging out with his friends from the neighborhood and his buddies on the football team (he is team captain). I wonder if that's healthy or normal.*

A: Yes, it's normal. Yes, it's healthy. That's the short answer.

Of course your son wants to spend more time with his girlfriend than with his old male friends—and not just for the newly discovered pleasures of kissing and hugging (and so on). The other reason, I'm guessing, is that he can talk to her in a way that he can't with his football and neighborhood pals. He can open up emotionally and have someone see that vulnerability as a good thing instead of as a fatal sign of weakness.

Kim Hays, the author of *Practicing Virtues*, a fine book on the similarities and differences between Quaker schools and military schools, tells a story about a boy in a military academy, a "powerfully built seventeen-year-old, [who] portrayed his girlfriend as his salvation: 'Being a leader you have a lot of pressure. . . . I started dating Karen and that helped me a lot. I had somebody to talk to, to share my problems with. Somebody to look after and care about me, I guess. . . . Before we got together, I used to keep my problems to myself. . . . Before, I just wanted to kill everybody, and now it's different.' "

I'm sure your son was not quite as tightly strung as this

young cadet, ready to explode with violence if he didn't get a chance to be tender with someone instead of tough and in charge all the time. But most boys face a similar struggle to appear more stoic, more unemotional, and less vulnerable than they really feel. With girlfriends, or even with female friends, they finally get a chance to show more of themselves— and that is a huge relief.

Think about how your son is with his male friends. I bet there is a lot of camaraderie, loyalty, and laughter but not a whole lot of heart-to-heart talking. Now think about how he is with his girlfriend. Did you ever imagine that he could spend that long talking to *anybody* on the phone? As one fourteen-year-old boy told me, "Guys are much more fun to hang out with. You can do crazy things with them. They don't care about anything. But girls are much better to talk to on the phone. You can't talk to a guy on the phone at all." He went on to tell me that girls gave him advice on clothes and style and how to be hip that his male friends never could have given him.

One interesting thing about this phenomenon is that it applies just as much to the boys who don't fit the stereotype of the strong, silent athlete as it does to the boys who do. I was anything but an athlete in school and avoided fistfights or wrestling matches like the plague. I knew I couldn't keep up with the bravado of the tougher boys, so I didn't even try. But even so, I was thrilled to finally have a girlfriend I could really talk to, someone who valued the aspects of myself that weren't so highly valued by the boy hierarchy on the playground—things such as being funny or smart or sensitive.

Since then I have listened to a lot of boys like your son. They all say the same thing—that when they have a serious girlfriend, at last they can talk to someone who will listen. They can be valued for a side of themselves that they usually have to hide.

My friend who teaches high school English tells a very similar story about these hypermasculine boys. In their last assignment of their senior year, when they are no longer going to have to face all their classmates in the hall or on the playing fields every day, they often turn in deeply moving and emotional essays, stories, or poems. The feelings they had been keeping under wraps can finally come out. The pressure to be cool is off—not cool in the sense of wearing the right shoes, but cool in the sense of not having any of those warm or hot emotions.

Of course, if your son is spending all his time with his girlfriend and none with his male friends, then she is presumably spending all of her time with him and none with her female friends. The appeal is the same as for boys: physical and emotional closeness. Like boys, some girls temporarily abandon their female friendships and put all of their time and energy into their romantic relationships. In fact, they often do more than their share of the "care and feeding" of the relationship, from initiating conversations to making plans.

The flip side of boys discovering their more tender emotions and the pleasures of heartfelt conversations is what many girls experience when they first have a serious boyfriend. Since they are used to free and easy and open communication with their female friends, girlfriends are often puzzled by their boyfriends' reluctance to talk. Boys and girls, who become strangers to each other in grade school as each gender discovers that the other gender has cooties, have to become reacquainted as teenagers. When this happens, boys may well let their male friends temporarily fall by the wayside. But they will come back together as deeper friends later, once the novelty has worn off and the guys have some practice with deep conversations.

Trying to Buy Friendship

Q: *My third-grade daughter, Caitlin, recently returned from a birthday sleepover with a brand-new Barbie, still in the box. She told me that every single girl at the party received one. "She had a whole stack of Barbie boxes, Mom," Caitlin said in amazement. But now she refuses to visit the child who gave her the doll, and tries to avoid her phone calls. I suspect she and her friends won't play with that child at school, either. What's going on?*

A: What's going on is an age-old strategy for winning friends and influencing people: the bribe. The problem is that bribes usually don't work when it comes to childhood friendships or acceptance. Most children are not above taking the bribe and then continuing to shun the one who tried the bribery trick—or even increasing the rejection, because now there's one more bad thing to say about this child during gossip time. I am assuming that the Barbie bribe you mention didn't create the rejection—usually children don't resort to bribes if they don't need to. But clearly the bribe didn't end the rejection, and it may have made things worse.

It's painful to imagine the conversation between the mother and the child as they planned this birthday party. Which of them was worried no one would come and suggested the Barbie bribe? Did either of them entertain the thought that people might come, take the Barbie, and ignore the underlying plea for friendship?

It's also painful to look back and remember those times when we may have tried this tactic for making friends ourselves, or when we took a bribe with no intention of following through with a friendship. I know I have awkward memories on both sides of this.

There are subtle and not-so-subtle reasons why this bribery technique doesn't work. The most obvious reason is that the bribe doesn't change any of the reasons for the child's rejection. You don't reject another child because she hasn't given you a good present lately! If the girl has been targeted for rejection because she is different in some way, or aggressive, or out of touch with the social rules, customs, and clothes of her peer group, none of that is changed by giving a gift.

A more subtle reason has to do with an area of social psychology known as attribution theory. One aspect of this theory is that we human beings don't automatically understand our own or other people's behavior. So we look for clues about why we act the way we do. In one famous study, researchers asked the subjects to do something they hated to do. Half of them were paid a tiny amount just for participating. The other half were paid a much larger sum of money.

Then the subjects were asked again how much they liked or disliked the activity. If they were paid a large sum, they still said they hated it. If they were paid only a small sum, they changed their tune and said they liked it.

Why? If you were paid a lot of money, you could look at yourself doing the activity you hate and tell yourself you're just doing it for the money. But if you weren't paid much at all, you had to ask yourself why you were doing this thing you hate. You don't want to think you're a dope, so you start to think that you must actually like the activity. Otherwise you wouldn't be doing it, right?

At your daughter's classmate's birthday party the guests could go to the party, get a doll, and go home and tell themselves (and their friends) that they only went in order to get a new Barbie. If they had gone to the party and hadn't gotten a bribe, they would have had to tell themselves that they attended because they wanted to.

I feel bad for the girl whose bid for acceptance was so roundly rejected. Sometimes the outcome isn't quite so bad. If a child isn't at the very bottom of the heap and tries to use bribery for a boost up a notch in the hierarchy, she isn't usually shunned. But she may be told in no uncertain terms that she's out of line. That can be humiliating, but children who learn their lesson this way are generally reaccepted by the group. But sometimes a child who tries to buy friendship can continue to be exploited—strung along by other kids who want the money and toys (and later, perhaps, the vacation trips and concert tickets). The child who makes all this stuff available to his "friends" may or may not be aware that he is being used. It may even be worth it for him. If he can't have friendship based on mutual respect and affection, he can at least have friendship based on exploitation. Or he may simply be oblivious and think that those partaking of his plenty are his real friends.

Sometimes it is parents who promote the attempt to purchase friendships. It may be that parents are so focused on material possessions that their child believes things are the only avenue to making a friend or expressing affection.

Socioeconomic status can play a role here too. When one child, or a few children in a class, are at a much higher income bracket than the rest of the kids, there can be serious repercussions in terms of friendship and acceptance. Wealthier students can get labeled as snobby or stuck-up, or can be seen as trying to bribe friends because they happen to have a trampoline or the coolest toys or the most lavish parties. In an odd way this is similar to the rejection of children who have less money than the rest of their classmates do. In one sense, rejecting children who already have so little in the way of material things is crueler. But from the point of view of psychological pain, both rich children and poor children experience the same sort of loneliness if they are rejected by their peers for being different.

I know I've been pretty harsh about this bribery issue. But there are variations on the theme that sometimes can be helpful. A friend of mine helped her daughter be better accepted by the crowd by having a special slumber party. There was no outright bribe, but the mother did some research to see what the other girls would really like to do. (She knew that her daughter wasn't in the loop about how to throw a great birthday party.) The mother made the invitations to the other parents, not the girls, enlisting the adults in aid of her daughter's acceptance. That way her daughter was not vulnerable to hostility or rejection from girls who might have laughed at the invitation. That party worked. The girl was more in sync with the other girls afterward and found a place for herself in the solid middle of the popularity hierarchy.

2

WHEN SOCIAL LIFE IS SCARY:
Children at Risk

The happy majority of children tumble out of the school bus, energetic and smiling, looking eagerly around to see their friends. But some enter school with their heads down, making almost no eye contact with other children. They slide alongside the groups of kids cheerfully talking. They head for their lockers. No one speaks to them, no one calls out to them to come over and share a joke. They enter the classroom and perhaps make conversation with a teacher. You can see the loneliness surrounding them like fog. The plight of these children is so painful that most adults don't, for emotional reasons, stay focused on them. It makes us feel too sad and helpless.

For most children, school is a positive social experience. For them, school is all about friends. It is the ideal arena in which to play a social game involving teammates, dear friends, enemies, fast-moving social cues, and exciting competition. In the kids' minds, their game is supervised from a distance by adults capable of preventing catastrophes—but they are rarely needed. Despite bumps and falls, the kids can manage most of their adventures on their own. And so each morning the majority cannot wait to resume the game. Indeed, they immediately renew conversations that were abandoned at three-fifteen the previous afternoon. Or they pick up the threads of phone, e-mail, and instant-message conversations that were under way last night when their parents told them to go to bed. They smile at one another, huddle together, touch each other, admire just-purchased clothes or basketball cards. They send each other the message "We recognize you. We're like you. We want to hang out with you."

All children are hungry for exactly that message. Some children hear it often; others almost never hear it. The ones that don't are socially starving in the midst of a crowd of children. And they are at risk.

Who are the children at risk? How do we identify them? What can teachers and parents do to help them? In our scene of the opening moments of school it seemed easy to distinguish between the haves and the have-nots of the social world. But in reality it can be difficult. Perhaps one of the popular kids is hurt and crying; perhaps two close friends are having a fight and one of them is devastated by it. Their pain looks like the pain of kids at risk, but it is much more transitory.

All children can get their feelings hurt; all children suffer losses and rejection. All children experience normal social pain. From a parent's point of view, of course, our own child's pain is serious, and it all breaks our heart, whether it is normal or not. So it can be very hard for parents to tell the difference between normal social pain and the kind of chronic rejection that puts children at risk. It is crucial, however, to distinguish between the two.

We have watched many parents overreacting to the

normal social pain of their children, and we have seen other parents who appear clueless about the plight of their at-risk children. We hope we can provide some categories and descriptions that will help parents make these distinctions.

Research conducted by John Coie at Duke University and Dan Olweus in Norway, along with that of many researchers who have followed in their footsteps, provides us with a foundation for understanding the makeup of a normal classroom. Even though almost all children experience bullying at one time or another in their school lives, 80 percent of children are not socially at risk; 20 percent are at risk. Who are the haves and who are the have-nots in a typical school?

Research tells us that 15 percent of a class is *very popular*. These are the trendsetters, the athletic and beautiful kids, the children whom other kids admire and want to emulate. They are not at risk for being lonely, because so many other children want to be with them. Will they be afflicted by many of the same doubts, insecurities, and confusions that all human beings are prey to? Of course. They are human. It is never easy being twelve or fourteen or sixteen, and growing up is not painless for anyone. But the very popular kids can be assured of having a lot of other kids with whom to discuss their struggles.

Forty-five percent of a classroom is made up of *accepted* children. An accepted child may have one best friend or several good friends, and feels a strong sense of belonging in a group. They too experience pain, rejection, betrayal, and anguish, of course, but not in the overwhelming quantities that would put them at risk. Why are they not overwhelmed by a betrayal from a friend? There are many reasons, the most powerful of which is that they have friends and a group identity to see them through their struggles. This is also true of the next 20 percent, the *ambiguous* children, who don't fall into any clear category. When researchers ask children, "Whom would you most like to be your friend?" unclassifiable children don't get many positive votes, but they don't receive many negative votes either. They share a lot of traits with children in the other groups. And they have that all-important protective factor: friends.

It is the 20 percent of children at the bottom of the social ladder who are potentially at risk. These are the neglected, controversial, and rejected children. The thing that they all have in common is that it is extremely difficult for them to make and keep friends. Without friends to stand at their side, these children are isolated and overlooked, or isolated and victimized. *Neglected* children (about 4 percent of the class) are often very shy or introverted. They are often bright and studious; they come to school not to socialize but to do the work. The popular and accepted kids may overlook them totally. These children are most often described as "falling through the cracks."

Controversial children are anything but invisible. They make up approximately 4 percent of a class, and they are well known. They have traits that are attractive to some kids and habits that drive other people crazy. A verbally fluent girl who becomes extremely popular and then turns cruel can become controversial (and ultimately rejected) by being too bossy or too exclusive. Children may declare about one— not all—of the popular girls, "She's stuck-up." If too many children get angry with her, that girl may be well on the way to becoming controversial. Hyperactive boys can be controversial. Many boys are attracted to their energy and boldness, but their impulsivity can irritate the class.

Rejected children (10–12 percent of the class) are the most at risk. Either no one wants to be their friend, or anyone who tries may risk getting teased alongside the rejected child. The ones with their heads down when they come into school, the ones who are trying to slip in under everyone's radar, are the *rejected-submissive* children. They put up with being rejected without much of a fight or protest. They often appear anxious or depressed; these are the children who turn up regularly at the nurse's office complaining of stomachaches or headaches that don't seem to have a physical basis. School is scary and stressful for them, and they don't seem to have any way to deal with their low status. Indeed, many rejected-submissive students lack social skills and are bewildered to find themselves so disrespected. One of the worst aspects of their problem is that these sad children are often disliked by teachers and other adults as well as by their peers—perhaps secretly disliked, because most teachers don't like to admit that there are students who rub them the wrong way. Children may see them as "easy targets," which leads to more victimization. Adults easily get annoyed with them as well. These children may even be seen as "getting what they deserve" when they are mistreated or tormented by the group or by a few aggressive children. Other times these social outcasts inspire a great deal of protectiveness in adults and a great deal of frustration when the protectiveness doesn't work. Sadly, often it does not.

Another subgroup of rejected children is labeled as *rejected-aggressive*. These kids fight back against their exclusion and rejection. Last year a man was arrested for a string of murders. According to a longtime neighbor of his, quoted in the *Boston Globe*, "He was an outcast [as a child] because he was mean and kids were mean back to him. . . . [He] was always a wild kid, other kids always picked on him." This quote reveals how hard it is to unravel the history of a rejected-aggressive child. Which came first, the rejection or the aggression? Was he rejected in the first place because he was impulsive and insensitive and frightened other children, or did he develop his pugnacious style as a coping mechanism for dealing with being excluded? It isn't always possible to tell.

Either way, children in this rejected-aggressive group, also called victim/bullies by some researchers, are needled and harassed by other children, often until they explode. Then they are the ones who get into trouble because their fury is often so extreme. Teachers overlook the provocation on the part of the group—we call it bearbaiting—because the reaction of the rejected-aggressive child is so much more obvious and dangerous. Rejected-aggressive children are caught in a Catch-22. They can't accept their rejection, but they make matters worse for themselves when they fight back. This dilemma undoubtedly contributes to the high incidence of mental disturbance in this group.

Children in the rejected-aggressive category run a serious risk of becoming bullies, delinquents, and criminals. Many of the high-profile cases of school shootings are likely to be children, usually boys, who fit this description of victim/bully behavior. They are rejected and tormented until they snap and escalate their revenge into extreme violent action. The humiliation they have experienced certainly does not excuse their aggressive response, but it may help to explain how children can take such drastic steps with such tragic consequences.

These categories—very popular, accepted, ambiguous, neglected, controversial, rejected-submissive, and rejected-aggressive—give more dimension to a class than one typically finds in discussions of bullying in school. Though there is a significant and important body of research on bullying, we prefer to use the term "social cruelty." Why do we make such a point of avoiding the word *bullying*? Because, in our experience, the moment you talk about bullies, the majority of parents think, "This doesn't apply to my child. He is basically a good kid." And so parents stop listening. It's always someone else's child who is the bully.

Our clinical experience with children in classrooms has led us to a different conclusion. We believe that at various times *all* children hold social power over other children, and therefore any child has the ability to hurt another child. At different times *any* child can engage in social cruelty, either by being aggressive or simply by laughing or watching some act of teasing. We believe that the large silent majority in a class exercises some control over the bullies in the classroom, either by watching passively as children are bullied or by making it clear which children are acceptable targets for bullying.

In videotaped studies conducted in Canada, it was found that 54 percent of children encouraged bullies by acting as interested spectators when one child was picking on another. Twenty-one percent imitated the bullying behavior by engaging in the same name-calling. Only 25 percent acted to intervene and stop the teasing. In other words, 75 percent of children either imitate or silently encourage classmates to pick on victims.

Different research studies on bullying, depending on how they define bullying, tell us that from 28 percent to 75 percent of children reported having been victimized in school. It is not true that "sticks and stones may break my bones but names can never hurt me." Name-calling and teasing are much more common than physical bullying in schools, and they are much feared by kids. Nineteen percent of children say they are chronically bullied, and 14 percent of kids have been, in the opinion of experts, traumatized by these experiences. These statistics are scary. At any given time, school can be an unsafe place for almost any child; it can be horrifying for children at risk.

It is essential that schools be aware of the potential harm that can come to children at risk during the ordinary school day. But it may offend our sense of the innocence of children to be on the lookout for social cruelty all the time. We don't want to think of schools as dangerous places—but for children at risk they certainly are.

Schools must have ongoing, systemwide programs to address social cruelty. Children need to be taught how to identify harassment and bullying and have close enough relationships with teachers that they will report dangerous or chronic acts of cruelty. Teachers need to be trained to discriminate between the healthy rough-and-tumble of children's social lives, which is likely to include some teasing and name-calling, and the chronic social cruelty that is practiced on children at risk. Guidance counselors must support the lonely and sometimes disturbed children who fill the ranks of the controversial, the neglected, and the rejected.

Parents must also act to protect their children if they fear they are being subjected to excessive social cruelty. The first thing that parents must do is face the fact of their child's lone-liness. Confronting their child's social isolation arouses so much pain in parents that some avoid it. Others—particularly mothers—think about nothing else and yet feel helpless to change their child's environment to make it possible for him or her to have friends. Parents must start by talking and lis-tening to teachers. Teachers have the evidence; they usually know who gets teased and which kids are alone for most of the day.

If a parent fears that her child is isolated, she needs to talk openly with school personnel and ask for their assis-tance. Then she needs to follow the recommendations of the guidance counselor. If the child lacks social skills, he or she may need to be in a group outside of school, a church group or Scouts or even a social skills training group, where the child can develop the skills to make friends. A guidance counselor may need to initiate discussion groups that will bring low-status children together in their own group for mutual support. Parents may need to change their social pat-terns and make more connections with other families that may open up friendship possibilities for their child. It is, in the end, the experience of having a loyal friend that can save a child's life.

The case studies that follow illustrate that adults can make a huge difference in the lives of children who are at risk. The first case study begins with a phone call familiar to every child psychologist—a parent's worry about a child's aggressive behavior. Jonathan gets the help he needs, and gets it early in life. The second case concerns a child whose isolation goes unnoticed through her childhood and adoles-cence because she is a fine student and follows the rules.

Only in adulthood is she able to seek on her own the friendship and professional help she needs. Both cases show how vital it is for parents and teachers to pay close attention to how children are doing socially, and take steps to help. When basic connections with friends and the group are absent it is very hard for children to learn the common language of social life.

CASE STUDIES

The Case of the Aggressive Preschooler

Jonathan's parents called toward the end of the summer, urgently asking for help with their son. It was just a few weeks before he was going to be leaving preschool to go to kindergarten, and he was having a terrible time of it. This was already his second preschool, and things were going from bad to worse. Jonathan had been asked to leave his first preschool because of aggressive behavior, and at his current preschool he had been sent home early several times for hitting or biting other children.

Jonathan's current school was reluctant to kick him out since he was scheduled to move on anyway, but they were at the end of their rope. Naturally—besides being concerned about his behavior in preschool and stressed about having to leave work early to pick him up—Jonathan's parents were worried about his upcoming adjustment to kindergarten. They didn't come out and say that they were also worried about him becoming a violent criminal, but I assumed that deep down they were anxious about that possibility. Aggressive behavior that goes above and beyond the ordinary pushing and shoving is unsettling for most parents, especially parents who are loving, caring, and nonviolent.

The first question to ask about aggressive children is exactly how much aggression we are talking about. Milder forms of aggression tend to improve on their own, or with a little bit of help from parents, teachers, or therapists. But somewhere between 4 and 8 percent of children have a more severe form of aggressive behavior. These more severe and long-lasting problems can be resistant to change and may need a major intervention. In fact, children with untreated severe aggression probably run the highest risk of any group of children. They are at higher risk for all types of criminal activity, drug abuse, dropping out of school, sexually transmitted diseases, unwanted pregnancy, and physical injury or death from fights and other dangerous behavior. With treatment, however, especially early intervention, many of these children can make a reasonable adjustment.

I asked Jonathan's parents what level of aggression they were hearing about. They reported a typical example: A girl called Jonathan a stinkyhead, and he pulled back his fist and walloped her good. He was sent home, where he alternated between promising never to do it again and insisting that he *had* to hit her because she was being so mean to him. The next day a different girl came up to the mom at pickup time and said, "Are you Jonathan's mom? He's bad."

That anecdote captures the difficulty of unraveling which came first, the aggression or the rejection. Wherever you start, there is an earlier layer. He hits because someone is mean to him, but they are mean because he is a hitter, but he's a hitter because no one likes him, and so on.

Jonathan, who is a bright kid, had his own understanding of this cycle of rejection and aggression. He told his mom that nothing would ever change until the other kids treated him better. And I am absolutely certain that, in their houses, the other children were telling their parents that they'd be happy to be nice to Jonathan if only he wouldn't be so mean.

As I gathered more information about Jonathan I learned that a neighbor boy down the street was not allowed to play with him, which Jonathan's parents thought was a huge over-reaction to some fairly mild and normal rough-and-tumble play between the two boys. I also learned that Jonathan did not just strike out impulsively in anger. He had a very long memory and would haul off and hit another child in the afternoon for something that child said or did earlier in the morning. On the other hand, 95 percent of the time he was a sweet, good kid with a doting mother and father.

The phone call I got from Jonathan's parents is one of the most common kinds of calls that a child psychologist receives. Some aggressive children are biters, kickers, and shovers. Some are verbally aggressive; others are bossy and intimidating. Some are mainly aggressive with siblings at home; others save their worst behavior for school. If they are a little older, they may exhibit a range of other antisocial behaviors, such as stealing, setting fires, being cruel to animals, and running away.

After just a few minutes on the phone with the parents of an aggressive preschooler, it is usually obvious that they either think their poor child is just misunderstood or fear that they have somehow spawned a little monster. So it's not surprising that some parents go on to ask if the therapist can help with the child's aggressive impulses, while others ask if the therapist can intervene with the school to help them stop overreacting to a perfectly normal kid. I call this problem "*Rashomon* in the nursery," after the famous Japanese movie in which the same crime scene is replayed four different times from the point of view of four different characters. In this case, there are at least two points of view, and sometimes more.

The solution to the *Rashomon* problem is to focus on very specific reports and observations instead of on global labels such as "aggressive." No child is aggressive in every single situation. Parents and teachers need to understand the sequence of events—everything that happens before, during, and after the aggression. Teachers need to understand parents' feelings of helplessness—feelings that lie behind much of their minimizing of their child's behavior. As one parent said, "I think [the preschool staff] are overreacting to normal behavior from a four-year-old boy, but apparently they don't think so, and since they have the power to throw him out, it doesn't really matter what I think." Of course schools can feel helpless too, which is why they often resort to expelling children whom they can't figure out how to handle effectively.

One of the main confusions for parents and teachers when dealing with aggressive behavior is the overlap between aggression and impulsivity. Some children are more impulsive than others are, and the trait may be genetic—in any event, it is often a tough thing to change. Impulsive children act immediately when they feel an urge, instead of stopping to think about it. If the urge in question is an aggressive impulse, then the child acts aggressively. It's important to figure out if a child is generally impulsive. Does he act out all his other impulses too, or is the acting out primarily aggressive?

Helping impulsivity means getting a child to insert some thought in between an impulse and an action. Theoretically, this is what time-outs and other punishments are meant to do—but they don't meet that goal. The only effective way to insert thought between impulse and action is to catch the child the moment before he or she acts out an impulse, which means more supervision. And you have to be quick!

The need for increased supervision may explain why some children are considered aggressive in preschool, while their parents, who keep an eye on them all the time, don't notice any problems. There just may not be enough one-on-one time in preschool to stop every aggressive impulse before it strikes. If you calmly interrupt impulsive aggressive behavior right before it happens, the child may reward you with a tantrum or by bursting into tears—or he may relax and move on to friendlier play.

A playful approach can help. Prevent the child from hitting a peer or smaller child, and then humorously say, "Pick on someone your own size!" This works especially well if you put up your dukes but then pretend to be afraid and run away—with him chasing after you giggling. That lets the child feel powerful without actually hurting anyone. Play can also slow things down and insert some thought in between impulse and action. Using dolls, stuffed animals, action figures, or trucks, first play out the sequence of having an impulse and acting it out. Then play out having the impulse and thinking it through. Another helpful activity is to have the child do some kind of rhythmic activity—jumping jacks, running, shouting—while you call out, "Slower, faster, louder, softer." That way the child learns to modulate behaviors and control impulses.

One trait that overlaps and gets confused with aggression is physicality. Some kids are just more physical than others are. If a child in preschool or kindergarten is more physical than his peers (and it's usually a boy), then he may feel like a fish out of water and be treated as such by teachers and other students. Some of these boys are bigger and stronger than everyone else, so when they just want to have fun and roll around, others see it as aggression or being out of control.

On the other hand, some children who are labeled as aggressive are physically active but clumsy and less coordinated than their peers. They may not mean to knock people over or step on their beautiful block constructions, but they just don't feel at home in their bodies. When they are yelled at or fussed at for being klutzy, they can easily retreat into isolation or, more likely, begin to really be aggressive to live up to their reputation.

For both physicality and impulsivity, it helps to do lots of wrestling at home. I mean playful wrestling, not the kind you see on TV. Research studies have shown that boys who engage in fun rough-and-tumble play with their dads are better at friendship than boys who don't. Of course, I recommend wrestling for moms too. Another helpful hint is to provide lots of opportunities for movement: dance, gymnastics, wrestling, running, bike riding, sledding, and so on. Practice yoga together for relaxation, self-control, and learning to move slowly and carefully. For a physically oriented child, school should include lots of running-around time, not hour after hour spent indoors sitting still.

Children who hit or hurt other children often have a particular deficit in either verbal skills or nonverbal skills. Those who have trouble putting their feelings into words can become very frustrated and resort to fists or angry outbursts to try to express themselves. Others—like Jonathan—have extremely high verbal skills and often feel superior to their peers. However, they also are easily frustrated because of their relatively poor social and physical skills.

When helping a child with aggression, it is very important to consider what specific skills he or she may lack. Does the child have trouble entering a group? Does he or she have trouble letting someone else take a turn? Does the child feel entitled to boss others around? Can he or she express needs and disappointments verbally?

Jonathan, it turned out, was only impulsive under very specific circumstances, when he felt frustrated or threatened. Because he was so verbal at other times, it was hard for his teachers to understand why he couldn't just "use his words." Children like Jonathan, who are verbally precocious but quite a bit behind their peers socially and nonverbally, are often misunderstood when they lash out because their high level of verbal, reading, and reasoning abilities makes it seem as if they should "know better." But sometimes good verbal skills can be a liability. For example, when Jonathan's mother confronted him with the school's reports about his behavior, he would argue like a masterful attorney, making a convincing case that he was merely restoring justice with his punch. His mother got nowhere with her insistence that, on the contrary, he was out of control and needed to learn to control himself. She tried to argue with him like a grown-up because he seemed to be able to argue at that level. In fact, he was emotionally very young, even younger than his years.

One of the things I like best about being a child psychologist is that development is usually on my side, but I get to take all the credit when the child's behavior improves. What I mean is that most aggressive preschoolers mature into less aggressive schoolchildren as they learn better verbal skills and better nonverbal social skills, develop a greater tolerance for frustration, and manage to better control their impulses. If they have been in therapy, it seems as though the therapy has done the trick, but more often it is just natural child development that does most of the work.

So with milder forms of aggression, we can usually let development take its course—as long as we protect other children, of course. For more severe forms of aggression, development may not be enough. An active intervention, especially if provided early enough, can make an enormous difference.

My sister Diane was visiting a day care center classroom that was having a lot of trouble with a boy, a biter. The staff told Diane that they had "tried everything," which meant they had tried every type of punishment. But they had never tried interrupting him *before* he bit someone, even though they told her they could always see it coming. While she was there they said, "Look, watch him now—he is about to bite that girl." They were going to let him do it and then try to think up some punishment or consequence to get him to stop. Instead, Diane rushed over, held the boy's head so he couldn't bite, and tried to make eye contact with him. He burst into tears, started yelling at her to let him go, and then cried some more. Eventually he spilled out a long, sad story about how he felt that no one at school liked him.

Most schools are a bit more on the ball than that, I think. But it is a challenge sometimes for parents to help schools appreciate the strengths of aggressive children instead of punishing them for being strong and active. The first step is for the parent and the teacher to be on the same wavelength about what is going on and what should be done about it. That's often difficult, because parents don't like to hear that their child is a bully, a biter, or a threat to other students. No one likes to hear that another parent has told *her* child not to play with *your* child. And teachers don't like to hear that they are imagining things or overreacting or that they don't know how to handle a specific child. Each person has to accept that the other one has a valid perspective to offer. Parents have to accept that the teacher is not imagining things, and teachers have to accept that their usual methods of handling aggression are not working.

One thing I always suggest to parents of aggressive children is that when you see aggression in a young child, look for trauma or fear. If a child is aggressive above and beyond the normal range, he or she may well have been a victim of or a witness to violence, or he or she may be scared inside. The aggression may be a front or a mask that helps the child feel more secure. Harsh punishments just make children feel less secure, and the cycle of aggression spirals out of control.

Happily, Jonathan's aggression subsided very quickly with therapy, though he continued to have some outbursts and some difficulties with peers. Overall, his adjustment to kindergarten was very smooth, and he was able to receive targeted help for his social and physical deficits while also receiving challenging schoolwork in keeping with his exceptional verbal abilities.

Sitting Alone at the Tea Party: A Neglected Child

When we look closely at children at risk, we see that most of them are actively disliked by at least some of their peers. They may be rejected outright and either submit to endless bullying or fight back angrily. Or they might be controversial, liked and disliked in roughly equal measure. But about 4 percent of children fall into a group that is called neglected.

This kind of neglect is not the same as neglect by parents, which is a form of child abuse that involves not meeting a child's basic needs. In fact, children who show up at school with no shoes or no coat or their hair uncombed are likely to stand out, while socially neglected children blend into the woodwork.

In terms of social relationships at school and in their neighborhoods, however, these children are indeed neglected. They are neither liked nor disliked, because no one knows them well enough to like them or dislike them. They participate very little in the social life of their school. Their classmates ignore them—not with malice, but because they don't notice them at all. Adults may not notice them either, because they are usually "good kids"—quiet, biddable, good students whose only fault is that they don't talk in class. Neglected children fall through the cracks. They don't get into trouble and they don't attract attention. They practically disappear.

Ruth, now an adult living in a Minnesota city, remembers a childhood that was pretty much bereft of friends. "When I was in the second grade my dad moved us from the city to my mom's family farm out in the western part of the state. We lived on the farm, but there were other houses not that far away," she remembers. "We lived on the lower road, and I knew someone from school who lived on the upper road. It was a short bicycle ride away. But during summer vacation, my mom kind of stopped us from visiting friends. I wanted to go, but my mom said, 'You just saw her. School just got out a month ago. And you'll see her in another month when you go back in the fall.' What sticks in my mind is that it was always such a big deal to go someplace with a friend or have someone over. So it just kind of didn't happen."

The roadblocks put in Ruth's way limited her social contact. She relates these memories matter-of-factly. They don't seem sad or painful to her; she's just telling it the way it was.

So the summer passed. "My mother was an extreme loner on the farm," Ruth says. "A family down the road would come over to visit maybe once a year or twice a year." Ruth pauses, thinking. "I have so few memories from then," she says. A shortage of childhood memories is common among children who are neglected socially, because most of us form our strongest memories with other kids—either enemies or friends.

Now in her fifties, Ruth says she finds herself amused by all the talk of play groups and play dates among contemporary parents. That was not part of her social world as a child.

When Ruth was in second grade she made an attempt at

a social life. It was a small tea party she had arranged for a few friends. "I can remember I was setting up a tea party and all the place settings were set, and kids were supposed to come over for tea." She pauses. "And Mom said, 'They're not coming.' And I remember thinking Mom had prevented the kids from coming." Looking back, Ruth thinks that her mother must have neglected to send out the invitations. "So no one came," she says. "I remember staring at Mother when nobody showed up. I knew she had had something to do with it."

After the move to the farm, Ruth flung herself into reading and TV. "I lived for TV," Ruth says, noting that she consumed a steady diet of 1950s and 1960s family shows—*My Three Sons*, *The Donna Reed Show*, *The Patty Duke Show*. "On TV, kids popped in and out of each other's houses all the time," she says. "I figured out what normal families were like by watching TV."

In school, where she was a good student, she remembers watching the other kids but not participating. "What I missed growing up is that I didn't have that interacting with other kids where you learn cues and how to connect with other people," Ruth says. "I was always a great observer, and I remember being envious. But I don't really remember a whole lot about social life at school. I don't remember going to parties. No dating. I was very timid back then. I wanted to join the girls' softball team, but I was too afraid to ask for permission from my parents. Dad was very meek and gentle, and my mother ruled the roost. Going home and getting the permission slip signed was too intimidating. I felt it wasn't worth the effort of being disappointed."

Today, as an adult, Ruth still has trouble making contact with others and in entering social groups. "I don't see friends informally on the spur of the moment. I still have that distance, and I have grown to accept it as normal."

After she graduated from high school, Ruth went to secretarial school and then to work.

"I didn't go to college until seven years after I graduated from high school," Ruth recalls. Her high school guidance counselor asked her about college, she says. But when she told him her family couldn't afford it, he ended the conversation. People who grew up with a solid circle of friends, and with parents who supported their goals and dreams, will have a hard time understanding how such an important decision could just slide by. The phrase "falling through the cracks" seems so passive, but ignoring a child so thoroughly takes some effort. "He should have done something," Ruth says. "I was so disappointed in him."

Later Ruth did go to college, attending the university where she had been working as a secretary. When she asked for her high school transcripts, she made a startling discovery. "We had a hundred and ten kids in my graduating class, and I didn't know until I saw it on my high school records that I was number three in my class." It is painfully ironic that if Ruth had not been such a good student, she might have come to the attention of the administrators, the counselors, or a special teacher and gotten some help with her social isolation.

In college Ruth became, as she puts it, "a little more social. It didn't take that much. I've always needed just a small number of friends. My mother had backed off once I was working full time. I established my adulthood." Not having the childhood and adolescent friendship experiences that most others have, she had to push herself to do things that seemed to come so naturally to others, and it is a tribute to her determination to be a part of the social world that she kept trying.

Even so, Ruth has found adult friendships difficult to make and to sustain. "It's sad not to have the natural interaction skills that so many adults have. I have tried so hard to get them. I've read books about how to start conversations, things like that. But there's still something a little odd about me."

The lacks in Ruth's life are striking—a lack of memories, a lack of connection, a lack of friends. But the saddest thing is the lack of effort on the part of adults to reach the child Ruth, to let her know that she was not invisible—that in fact she was the third-ranked student in her class and someone who was eager to be a good friend.

Teachers can make a remarkable difference in the lives of neglected children, and they often do. In fact, there are many times when the life of a neglected child is saved by the love and attention of a caring teacher, coach, or Scout troop leader. Good teachers work all the time to make connections with kids and to connect kids with others. There are guidance counselors all over the United States who serve as anchors for neglected kids. Often the attention of a single caring adult who talks to neglected children, looks them in the eye, and notices that they're there can set those kids on the road to sociability. Such teachers provide coaching until children find that one invaluable connection—a friend.

In college, Ruth discovered people with interests similar to hers and started having a social life—although it was never easy. Some neglected children begin to make these connections in high school, when the extreme conformity of middle school begins to wane.

But the risks of social neglect are very high. Extreme social isolation can lead to depression and even suicide.

When a young girl who had been a student at one of America's large suburban high schools committed suicide last fall, her fellow students were devastated. The dead girl's face—tentatively smiling from among her classmates in her homeroom picture—appeared on the front page of the local paper. Adults and students alike protested that they had had no indication that the girl was sad or depressed. She had left no notes, showed no signs, talked to no one. As counselors looked deeper into this girl's death, they realized something chilling: No one remembered much about her at all. No one appeared to have known her. No one. None of the girls in her class had been friends with her. No one remembered sitting with her on the bus. No one even remembered sitting next to her in class. Even her teachers had only fuzzy recollections. "She was very quiet," one said. "She never caused any trouble," said another. It was as if the dead girl had been invisible when she was among them.

It's hard to imagine that children can disappear so completely, even in a huge high school. But this girl did. We will never know if loneliness was the cause of her suicide or if it just added to a hidden burden of pain that she could no longer bear. But we do know that not being known is in itself a terrible burden to bear.

QUESTIONS & ANSWERS

Learning Nonverbal Language

Q: *My son is very bright, but when it comes to social interactions he just doesn't seem to get it. He's always a step behind and a little bit off-kilter. This leads to a lot of frustration, since he can't understand why other kids don't seem to want to play with him. How can I help him?*

A: There are many, many reasons why children don't fit in. They might be aggressive, or excluded because of a difference in appearance or culture. But some children seem to have a specific deficit in nonverbal communication—interpreting body language, reading facial expressions, picking up subtle cues from other people, and so on. This is a deficit that applies to many children who end up rejected by their peers. In their book *Helping the Child Who Doesn't Fit In*, psychologists Stephen Nowicki Jr. and Marshall Duke provide a useful model for understanding and helping children who have trouble using and understanding nonverbal communication.

These difficulties can come from various sources: a lack of social experience, problems with early attachment to a primary caregiver, learning disabilities, or emotional distress. If a child grows up in an isolated household or moves so frequently that he never gets a chance to make friends, he might miss out on learning about nonverbal forms of communication. Some children have a highly developed verbal intelligence but are less adept at nonverbal aspects of intelligence, including social and emotional interactions. Others may have a neurological disorder, such as Asperger's syndrome, that interferes with the ability to make social connections. Depression or anxiety can also interfere with the ability to pay attention to important features in the social environment or to get an accurate picture of what other people are saying or feeling.

Whatever the cause, Nowicki and Duke propose a practical, skills training approach to solving the problem. They break down their program into four basic steps. Each requires awareness of the problem, practice, and application to real-life situations.

- **Discrimination of nonverbal cues**—for example, being able to tell the difference between different facial expressions. This can be practiced with pictures from magazines by asking the child to sort them according to facial expressions. In a real-life situation, you can ask a child what he or she thinks a person might be feeling.

- **Understanding the meaning of nonverbal cues**—for example, learning which facial expressions go with which emotions. Children can practice naming their own emotions and recognizing the physical signs of different emotions, such as butterflies in the stomach or sweaty palms for nervousness. You can ask them to name the emotion that might go with various situations, such as getting a present, losing a favorite toy, and so on.

- **Meaningful expression of specific nonverbal cues**—for example, knowing that a smile can help when entering a new group. Children who have trouble with nonverbal communication often don't realize what they are communicating to their peers nonverbally. Such children may come over to a group and ask to play, but their body language comes across as angry or contemptuous. They might not know how to show that they like someone or that they are pleased to be included in a game. To practice this skill, ask a child to demonstrate various emotions and intentions without words, using only facial expressions and body language.

- **Application of nonverbal cues to social situations**—for example, have the child watch TV with the sound off and guess what the characters are feeling and what they might do next, or have the child role-play entering a group or asking a classmate to join in a game or project.

In addition to these strategies suggested by Nowicki and Duke, I would recommend a few more activities for the child with nonverbal communication deficits. Playful wrestling, or rough-and-tumble play, is a great way for kids to learn subtle nonverbal cues, as long as it is done with safety in mind—no professional wrestling moves! The constant physical interplay of wrestling gives lots of practice in nonverbal communication. Because these children are still learning about nonverbal messages, it helps to have a code word that means "Stop!" so that the wrestling doesn't get out of hand. I like to use code words that are kind of funny, like *banana* or *zirkle*, because that adds an element of silliness and also makes a bridge between language and the nonverbal aspects of wrestling.

Children who struggle with nonverbal communication often tend to avoid eye contact, so games such as a staring contest where you stare into each other's eyes until one person laughs or smiles are fun and helpful. Or find a book of acting exercises and try some. They're excellent for teaching nonverbal communication. Better yet, see if your child wants to be in a play. Put on skits at family gatherings, and coach the child to use broad facial expressions and gestures that really get the point across. Activities such as dance, gymnastics, martial arts, drawing, sculpture, and team sports all provide good practice for nonverbal communication as well.

When a Child Is Sadistic

Q: *I have a student who lies, manipulates, and can be very cruel. The thing that worries me most is that it seems to give her satisfaction. How can I help her soften up her feelings?*

A: You are right to worry most about this child's behavior giving her satisfaction. If you had not mentioned that, I would probably have focused my answer on the fact that every child—every single one—experiments with social power. Every child tries out lying, manipulating, teasing, dominating, and betraying. These experiments are similar to the way that every toddler drops food off the high-chair tray to experiment with gravity and with getting a reaction from his or her parents.

Most children learn fairly quickly that it isn't really worth it to make these social experiments into habits. They lose too many friends that way, and they may quickly be shunned by the group. They might still resort to lying or manipulation in special situations, but they don't make it a way of life.

But some children develop a taste for manipulation. They begin to mistreat their peers not just to see what will happen but for pleasure. If they aren't helped to get back on a better social track, being cruel can become an ingrained part of their personality. Then, as they have fewer and fewer positive interactions with their peers, they can become more and more deeply entrenched in that role. Finally the only way left for them to interact is as a tyrant or a back-stabber.

I think that most deliberately cruel behavior is done by children who either feel bad or are trying hard not to feel bad. Either way, they feel better when someone else feels bad, and that's where the satisfaction comes in. Unfortunately, that satisfaction can easily develop into sadistic pleasure in causing other people harm.

Do these words seem too harsh to apply to a young child? No one likes to use the word *sadistic* about a child. But sadism is simply taking pleasure from inflicting pain on others—and children sometimes do that. The targets of their cruelty have no trouble seeing it as deliberate. But children don't ever go home and say to their mom or dad with a diabolical laugh, "Guess what I did to Susie today—I made her cry and run to the teacher three times. She was like putty in my hands." Instead, children paint a picture of themselves as the helpless victims of mean children and adults who are out to get them. Many parents, and even teachers, feed into this selective reporting, comforting the child with phrases such as "They're just jealous of you because you're so smart and strong and popular."

Another reason why habitual cruelty can be hard to break is that it "works." What I mean is that it has its rewards, even if it has negative consequences too. If you feed off people being scared of you, sucking up to you, or bursting into tears because of you, then you will be well fed if you continue the behavior—even if the adults punish and scold you for it.

Sometimes it works even better than that. I consulted in one first-grade classroom where the rest of the girls were so desperate to be in one girl's good graces that they handed over to her the power to make them all miserable. She would play one against the other, leaving them all anxious and traumatized. In another classroom the queen bee actually wore a plastic tiara to school, and most of the other girls lived or died based on whom she favored that day and whom she dismissed. She didn't even have to say the magic words "I'll be your best friend." Her power was beyond mere words.

So to socialize a child who has made a habit out of lying and manipulating her peers, we have to make it less of a victory. Unfortunately, children with these habits don't usually respond well to punishments. During a time-out, for example, they are more likely to be planning their revenge than pondering how to be a better person. During a stern talking-to they are more likely to be planning how they will report this cruel abuse to their mother than taking it to heart ("The teacher yelled at me for no reason").

So instead of adding new punishments, the goal is to make antisocial behavior less rewarding. One of the best ways to do this is to help the other children stand up for themselves and each other, and to develop solid friendships among them that can withstand the pulls of a socially gifted manipulator or tyrant. The tricky part is not to encourage the other kids to gang up on the overly powerful child in such a way that she then becomes the new scapegoat.

I have seen deposed queens withdraw from their schools, with many parents and teachers cheering, forgetting that there is a hurt little girl inside the cruel or manipulative shell. The alternative, which I will grant is a lot more difficult, is to help that child back into the fold, to help her be part of the moral and ethical community. In the meantime, you also have to interrupt the destructive behavior as much as possible, to call her on it, let her know that you notice it and you don't approve, that you expect more kindness and cooperation and teamwork.

The girl you describe needs a crash course in empathy. But can empathy be taught? It can. Empathy is a complex combination of thoughts and feelings, and it can indeed be taught, coached, and encouraged. For some children, a question such as "How would you feel if Chrissy did that to you?" may be all that is needed as an opening for teaching empathy. Whenever someone in class is sad or has their feelings hurt, you have a teachable moment for developing empathy and kindness.

But for other children—and I suspect your student falls into this category—that basic approach just falls flat. She's happy to have the other person feel bad. That means that she has successfully passed off her rotten feelings to someone else in a game of emotional hot potato. If you point out that Jimmy is crying, she will think, "Better him than me."

Or at least she will see that she has shared her rotten feeling, creating company for her misery.

So the children most in need of empathy training are the most resistant to it. They may need a more targeted intervention, such as individual or group therapy, if the behaviors have really become entrenched.

I was struck by your saying that you would like to help this girl "soften up" her feelings. At the risk of sounding too much like a touchy-feely psychologist, sometimes all a child needs is a bit of love and attention. This gives her the strong internal belief in her own value to allow her to develop good friendships and effective skills for being a part of the group instead of a cruel ruler or a back-stabbing outsider.

You can help too, by establishing a classroom environment that supports moral behavior. Your school should have an ethos and a moral code that stand against excessive social cruelty. In her book *You Can't Say You Can't Play*, Vivian Paley describes how she put up a sign in her kindergarten class that proclaimed You Can't Say You Can't Play. At first it was greeted with disbelief. "What's the whole point of playing?" one student wailed.

Paley did not stop exclusion in kindergarten that year. But every time a situation arose she was able to ask the children whether their behavior lived up to the classroom rules—and generated a moral discussion as a result. She concluded that her rule was a "ladder out of the trap we've been in"—it helps children get out of the "habit" of exclusion. Any moral stand, any code of conduct posted at the front of a classroom helps children out of the trap of their own meanness. That's what your student needs.

How Can Two Kids from the Same Family Be So Different?

Q: *My two sons couldn't be more different. One is a leader in every way, well liked and well respected by peers and adults. My other son has friends and is a sweet boy, but he can be impulsive and definitely can rub people the wrong way—sometimes even his closest friends. I can't believe that these two guys came from the same basic mix of genes and grew up in the same house. What makes them so different?*

A: A great variety of factors go into making a child a social leader rather than one of the pack, or making one child a solid member while another is controversial.

One of the most important factors when it comes to social skills and social success is the level of a child's impulsivity. Not enough of it? A child is left out of the social whirl. Too much? A child may be entertaining for a while but also spells trouble and eventually may be avoided or shunned by other kids. Just as in so much else in life, a moderate amount of impulsivity is best.

Think about a playground at recess. A moderately impulsive child suggests a game and the other moderately impulsive children follow along happily. Meanwhile, a low-impulsivity child sits alone on the bench, too timid to participate. At the other extreme, a highly impulsive child calls, "Let's see if we can climb up onto the roof and jump off. It's not so high, and the teachers aren't looking." His peers may think he's funny, they may think he's headed for big trouble, or some of both. But they're unlikely to follow him into his wild, risky play.

So if moderate impulsivity is best, why don't all children have a moderate amount? Why is there such a range? The answer may be that we are social animals and the group as a whole benefits from having a range of tactics and a range of levels of impulsiveness.

I wish I could say I made up that theory, but in fact it comes from some interesting research into monkey behavior. Lynn Fairbanks, of the University of California at Los Angeles, studies impulsivity in vervet monkeys, small primates that live in colonies. Her technique involves placing a new monkey, a stranger to the colony, in a small cage inside the larger enclosure where the other monkeys live. She has found that—just as with humans—the vervet monkeys showed a wide range of impulsive behaviors in response. The most impulsive ones raced over to the "intruder," sniffed it, and even stuck their fingers into the cage to touch the unfamiliar monkey. That's a risky strategy for these individual monkeys, because they really don't know how friendly or aggressive the new monkey might be. But you can see how it helps the group to have a few monkeys who take this kind of risk. The impulsive monkeys don't worry about danger and therefore gather a great deal of useful information for the colony as a whole.

Other monkeys, those very low in impulsivity, also serve an important function for the group. By watching from the sidelines and keeping themselves out of harm's way they make sure that someone lives to tell the tale if the intruder turns out to be dangerous. In between these two extremes are the moderately impulsive animals, not totally cautious but not reckless either. These monkeys turned out to be the highest-status monkeys, the alphas. We can think of them as equivalent to your student-leader son.

It makes sense that the moderately impulsive monkeys (and children) are the most successful socially. Members of the group with a very high level of impulsivity eventually will alienate everyone or will engage in so much risky behavior that no one will want to follow them. Those with extremely low impulsivity are not likely to be effective leaders because they prefer caution to taking initiative.

If we look at the group as a whole, we can see why it helps to have some people who are very impulsive, some who are not impulsive at all, and some who are right in the middle. Each level has its payoffs and drawbacks.

Highly impulsive children get a lot of attention. Everyone watches them to see what will happen when they test the limits. But that attention is not the same as friendship or acceptance by the group. The same qualities that make an impulsive child interesting can also make him or her untrustworthy and risky to be friends with. A child at the other end of the spectrum, however, may never get enough attention from the group to show off his or her best qualities, and thus loses out on friendships and group status.

Will your sons' impulsivity traits change over time? Your impulsive son will learn to manage his impulsivity better as he grows up, but it will likely remain part of his personality. In her research, Fairbanks found that high or low impulsivity was consistent over time, suggesting that it is an enduring personality trait, not just a result of how adventurous a monkey was feeling that particular day. Development plays a part as well. Adolescent monkeys were more likely to be highly impulsive (like adolescent humans).

Generations of parents and schools have discovered that you can't punish or scold highly impulsive children into being less impulsive. What we can do is provide more supervision and encourage social leaders to keep an eye out for their peers or—in this case—their brothers.

Talking About Personal Hygiene

Q: *I'm a fifth-grade teacher and I have a really unpleasant problem in my class this year. It's about Rosie. Puberty has hit this girl hard, but her personal hygiene has not kept up. To put it bluntly, she smells. Her body odor is quite offensive. The other kids don't like to sit anywhere near her. In fact, they drag their desks away from hers when she sits down. This has been going on long enough so that Rosie has become almost totally isolated socially. I hate to admit it, but I find myself pulling away from her too, though I know I should intervene somehow. What do you suggest?*

A: The only thing I can suggest is a difficult conversation with Rosie and an equally painful conversation with her parents. You have to find a private place and a quiet moment when you can ask Rosie, "Kids tease you, don't they?" She'll probably look acutely uncomfortable and nod. Then you'll have to plow ahead by saying, "Has anyone ever talked to you about what they're saying?" She will likely shake her head and start to cry.

"Are you aware that as girls start to grow up and their

bodies develop, they need to shower more? Do you know why?" Rosie will nod, and you will ask, "Can you tell me why?" She will say, "Because I sweat so much."

Once Rosie acknowledges that she knows what the issue is, you can begin to ask further questions: "Have you talked about this with your mom?" "Has she talked about body odor with you?" "Do you shower every day?" "Do you use deodorant?" If you get more acknowledgment, you must begin to support her by talking about other fifth graders you have known who have suffered from this problem.

Perhaps, if you are so inclined, you could share some anecdote from your own life, about your discomfort with your own body as you were growing up. I cannot dictate what you should do. It needs to be something authentic, personal, and from your heart. You can do it with personal anecdote; you can do it awkwardly, gracefully, or with a science lesson included. But you must do it. Why? You are the only adult witness, both to Rosie's body odor and to the rejection of her by the other children. If you don't intervene and help Rosie, her life in school will become worse and worse.

We can't know why Rosie hasn't attended to herself. We don't know if it is a family issue; perhaps she doesn't have access to the bathroom or her parents have a rule about not showering too frequently. We don't know if Rosie has some self-consciousness about developing into a woman and her defense against her own anxiety is to ignore her body. We don't know whether her mother is uncomfortable with having a grown-up daughter and is embarrassed to talk to her. She may come from a culture in which bathing and deodorant use are not as prevalent as they are here in the United States—in which case you or the school nurse might have to

buy the deodorant and give it to Rosie, along with instruc-
tions about using it. The only thing we can be sure of is this:
If no one talks to Rosie, she will be increasingly rejected by
the other children in the class.

How can I be so certain about Rosie's rejection by her
classmates? Because I have seen it happen many times. Children are acutely aware of each other's bodies. After all, they
spend hours a day working closely with each other at desks,
standing closely in the lunch line, and perhaps changing in
front of other kids after PE class. School can be a pretty intimate place. Middle-school children are also, for psychological and hormonal reasons, tuned in to each other's physical
development. Nothing escapes them: breast development,
acne, and everything else get noticed.

Because the pressure to be like other children is so
strong among elementary- and middle-school kids, anyone
who is different will produce a reaction in the mainstream
kids and may be excluded. Children with tics, Tourette's
syndrome, or strange compulsions may be marginalized by
the majority. Classmates may be afraid of a child who is in a
wheelchair or of someone with cerebral palsy whose body
looks distorted. Students will almost certainly need support
in order to overcome their inhibitions about approaching
someone whose disability makes them so different.

However, children can distinguish between correctable
problems and problems that cannot be helped. Though they
might be inhibited about befriending someone in a wheelchair, they will be ruthless about criticizing someone who
doesn't shower. And once you have a reputation for not
showering, you are socially doomed. I have heard tenth
graders still referring to a former sixth-grade classmate as

"the girl who didn't shower." Kids have long memories for these things.

I would say that it is almost impossible to come back from such a reputation once you are stuck with it, but a teacher in South Carolina once told me about how a group of teachers resurrected the social life of a disabled fourth-grade boy who smelled of feces. This boy, who came from a significantly poorer family than his classmates, suffered the misfortune of being born without a rectum. After surgery performed in infancy, he had a colostomy tube that emerged from his body and a plastic bag to hold the fecal matter. The teachers had been told about that, but they and the children were acutely aware that he smelled like feces. The teachers tried to ignore it and organize their class in the usual way, but the children were not shy about telling adults, "He smells," or whispering to one another, "He smells like shit."

Eventually a teacher investigated the matter closely and found that because of his acute self-consciousness, the boy was not wearing the bag, but rather was stuffing the tube with paper towels in hopes of stopping the smell. His attempt to fix the problem was making it much worse. The teacher took him to the nurse; the nurse contacted his parents and gave them and the boy additional training in how to manage the colostomy bag. His teacher both reminded him and helped him to change the bag, and in time he did not emit the odor he had before.

Unfortunately, his classmates still were not willing to risk being his friend or even get physically close to him. So the teachers created an incentive program for the other children—specifically the boys—to get to know him again. The boy was a good basketball player, and so the teachers gave him "medical privileges" to go play basketball during a free period and allowed him to take a volunteer to play with him. As long as another child volunteered to accompany him, both were allowed to leave class and go to the gym. This obvious incentive system, which some people might regard as a bribe, worked very well. There were enough boys who wanted to get out of class to volunteer, and gradually the act of playing basketball with this boy helped bring him back into the mainstream.

This story has a truly happy ending because the physician father of one of the children in the class heard about the boy's dilemma and knew of a corrective surgery that would create a new rectum for him. This father took responsibility for getting the boy to the appropriate surgeon and for helping to raise the money to pay for the surgery, and so the problem was corrected. When the teacher told me this story she cried as if there had been a miracle. But to my mind, the miracle began with the teacher.

Teachers are witnesses to the cruel treatment of some children by other children. They also, because of their closeness to the kids, know *why* some children are excluded. And so it is with Rosie. If you as the teacher do not act, if you are too frightened and inhibited, the child will experience systematic and chronic rejection. Now, I know that this goes beyond the job description for a teacher; I know that teachers are not specifically trained for this kind of work. Fair enough. You can ask for support from the nurse or other health professionals if you are too uncomfortable to discuss body odor with a fifth-grade girl. But you must act.

Finally, I know that teachers are often afraid how parents will react when they discuss something personal with their child. If a teacher worried about the consequences of having the conversation about showering that I proposed earlier—and I know that teachers today live in fear of parental criticism and lawsuits—then it would be important to get the support of an administrator. You might say, "I am going to have a conversation with Rosie about body odor and showering. Will you speak to the parents on my behalf, or will you back me up if I speak to the parents and they become upset? I need your support in order to do this, but it is essential that I speak to her about the problem, because if I don't, the whole class will turn against her." Speaking to Rosie, contacting her parents, getting the support of administrators—all of these things are my definition of courage on the job.

The Roots of Bullying

Q: *Were all bullies bullied themselves when they were younger?*

A: I am so glad you asked that question, because it allows me to tell the story of a Spanish play written about three hundred years ago by Pedro Calderón, which is one of the few things I still remember from high school. The play is called *La vida es sueño*, or *Life Is a Dream*. It's about a benevolent king who hears a prophecy that his young son will be a cruel tyrant when he succeeds his father and takes over the throne. The king loves his people so much that he can't bear for this to happen. But he also loves his son, so he does not know what to do. His councilors pressure him to kill his son to prevent the calamity. The father cannot bring himself to do this, so he locks the prince in the deepest dungeon.

There the boy grows up, mistreated, underfed, poorly clothed, miserable, and alone.

Years later someone prevails on the king to reconsider. Perhaps the prophecy was mistaken, or perhaps the years in the dungeon have taught the young man a lesson that will prevent him from being a cruel king. While the prince is asleep, soldiers dress him in royal robes and put him on the throne. When he wakes up, everyone treats him as though he is indeed the king and has just woken up from a nap. The courtiers and advisors dismiss his confusion as the result of bad dreams. He proceeds, of course, to be a cruel king, thus fulfilling the prophecy. What else would anyone expect, given his prolonged mistreatment and his confusion? The real king, watching from the side, is horrified at his son's brutality. When the prince falls asleep his father has him taken back to the dungeon. When the prince wakes again he is not sure what was a dream and what was real.

I think this story provides a metaphor for the cycle of brutality when children—usually boys—are placed by society into positions of power after having been abused. I am thinking of the boarding-school hazing by older boys of younger boys, who then pass on the hazing once they become upperclassmen, or the big kids in the neighborhood beating up the smaller kids, who then continue the tradition of violence once they grow older, or children who are abused by parents and then left in charge of their younger siblings.

These children—again, especially boys—are given few if any opportunities to heal from the psychological trauma of having been bullied. They usually can't cry about it or talk about it with a sympathetic listener, because those healing avenues are closed to kids who have to present themselves as tough. They may not have anyone in their lives who can support them and encourage them not to pass that aggression along to the next victim. It's easy to see how a bullied child would become a bully, or how a victim of aggression might be generally aggressive. Left to their own devices to find a way to get rid of those aggressive impulses inside, children take them out on anyone who makes a likely target—usually the kids who are smaller and weaker.

Not every bullied child, however, becomes a bully in turn. Sometimes a bullied child might have his or her spirit broken and become a permanent passive victim instead of a bully. The bullying might be so relentless, with the child always one down, that there is no chance to pass it on to someone else. Or the child might be so intimidated and fearful that he responds to his own victimization with a big Kick Me sign on his back instead of with a swagger of defiant toughness.

Other times, usually with the help of a supportive adult, a bullied child breaks the cycle and chooses not to pass it on. In my work with adult men who were physically and sexually abused as children, I heard this powerful story over and over. Despite all that had been done to them, or perhaps because of what was done, they retained a strong moral conscience and chose not ever to hurt anyone else the way that they were hurt. Usually this positive outcome is helped along by a supportive listener—often a teacher, coach, or relative—who helps the child see that there is a world beyond the limited choice of being a bully or being a victim.

But all that still doesn't answer your question about whether every bully was once a victim of bullying. Being bullied certainly helps to train a bully, both by modeling and by filling the victim with anger and the desire for revenge. But some bullies seem to be self-taught. Like every other child, they push and shove a little, jockeying for position in the group. But perhaps they knock over someone who is a bit fragile, and that child bursts into tears instead of shoving back. And perhaps the one who gave the push gets a strong feeling of power and prestige from that encounter and decides to pursue that kind of interaction as a way to feel good about himself, maybe even as a way to feel superior to everyone else. Then we see the birth of sadistic cruelty (either a mild case or a severe case, depending on many other factors) without the child having been bullied beforehand by an angry father or a mean brother or a tough kid in the neighborhood.

I think self-taught bullies are rare, however. Most kids learn to be mean by experiencing or watching meanness. If we break the cycle and prevent one child from being bullied, or help one child heal from the terrible effects of bullying, we can prevent a whole new generation of victims.

A Girl Gang

Q: *I watched a group of seventh-grade girls at the school where I teach—they call themselves a "gang"—insult and tease a boy for months. Finally, when he was with a friend, the two boys wrote sexual insults about the girls on a Web page. For being the coauthor of those insults, he and his friend were accused of harassment and suspended from school for three months. Meanwhile the girls were treated as helpless victims. The girls had gotten what they wanted: The boy they didn't like was kicked out of school! The fact that his friend* *was suspended too was just a bonus. The girls' power was in-credible. I thought the girls set up the boys, and the adults harshly punished the boys. What could I have done to help the boys, or to convince the adults that the girls were guilty too?*

A: The idea of a gang of powerful, vengeful girls with no sense of guilt is hard for us to accept. Why? The reasons are cultural. Don't you believe, deep down, that girls are just a little bit nicer than boys? Aren't girls supposed to be made of "sugar and spice and everything nice"? Come on, aren't men responsible for most of the murder, rape, and violence in the world? Doesn't that prove that women are fundamentally more moral than men?

I cannot provide a definitive answer to these philosophical questions. Indeed, I have struggled and will struggle with these questions all my life. But I do know how people generally answer the question about girls being more moral than boys because I have posed it to audiences many times. Though they are loath to acknowledge their bias, most people say yes, girls are just a bit more moral than boys are and do a bit less harm than boys do.

If that is our stereotypical view of girls, our romanticized notion of girlhood, then no wonder it's hard to understand girl gangs and their raw use of power. We come up against our own cultural assumptions when we try to discern what girl gangs are up to. We just don't have the internal models of girl cruelty that we have for boy aggression. Back-stabbing and gossiping might fit our profile for girls being mean, but systematically driving a boy to the edge? No way.

Boys use power in a much more obvious way than girls

do. Boys beat each other up; they grab at girls' bodies; they commit acts of vandalism. Typical boy behaviors, as well as our cultural beliefs, propel us to conclude that boys are probably guilty until proven innocent. Meanwhile, girls are usually considered innocent until proven guilty. Boys are aware of this inequity, and girls are too. Teachers, however, are in a position to comment on the relative cruelty of boys and girls in the social arena. What they have to say may surprise many people.

Whenever I work with elementary- or middle-school faculty, the teachers report to me that girls are meaner than boys are. The teachers describe how girls gossip about, double-cross, betray, and exclude other girls. It is girls who say about another child, "She smells. She doesn't shower," and then discuss their victim day after day in a relentless and unforgiving way. I have read notes written by seventh-grade girls sizing up boys physically in a way that we usually think only boys do about girls. These notes describe the hygiene, looks, eyes, and even pubertal development of boys so graphically that it made me acutely uncomfortable. My thought was, "Thank God I'm not in class with these seventh-grade girls! They're tough."

I think almost every seventh grade contains a group of girls who are a potentially dangerous gang. All they need in order to be freed from the restraints of civility is a leader who is angry or vengeful, who has suffered from disinterest, neglect, or abuse in her family, or who is corrupted by the admiration of her peers.

All children experiment with social power. All children, boys and girls, experiment with exclusion, with hurting the feelings of others. What, then, stops a group from engaging in extremely cruel behavior? Why don't these experiments run wild?

Sometimes they do. But what stops children from excessive cruelty most of the time is either the underlying mental health and moral foundation of the kids themselves or the protective environment around them. Good schools monitor the activities of children so that they cannot engage in relentless cruelty.

However, when the environment is biased and people are predisposed to see boys as more troublesome than girls, two things are likely to happen. Girls will act more like gangs, and boys who retaliate will be treated unjustly by adults. That's what happened in the case you describe. Because the two boys were seen as sexual harassers, their crime was judged much more harshly than was the girls' verbal provocation. With the benefit of hindsight, we can see what you saw: The girls were relentless and remorseless. They were not punished for what they did to the boys day after day, but the boys were punished for what they did in one impulsive moment. And the reason is cultural. Because rapists are men, boys are sometimes seen as potential rapists. Because girls are seen as the victims of men's sexual violence, their own cruelty is often overlooked. This does not mean that girls or women ask to be sexually assaulted or harassed. It does mean, though, that when our society passes out blame and identifies victims, there is a bias toward seeing the boys as perpetrators and the girls as victims.

There are things a teacher could do in this situation, but they require persistence and courage. You would have had to take the girls on as they were tormenting the boys. You would have had to identify their behavior, speak to them about it, alert other faculty members to it, and possibly speak to their parents about how mean they were. Your perceptions might have met with skepticism on the part of your colleagues or the parents. Girls tormenting boys? Your colleagues know it is possible, but your observation still runs counter to our cultural assumptions about girls. You'd have had to emphasize that these particular girls are definitely not made of "sugar and spice." You might have had to make the case that "these girls are mean. They have no mercy. They think of themselves as a gang and they act like a gang. The boys can't handle them and are overwhelmed and angry. Eventually the boys are going to strike back, and it's going to be ugly."

Once you had put your colleagues on alert, the data on the girls' behavior would have started pouring in, and the girls would have begun to modulate their behavior. Unfortunately, what actually happened is that the boys went public with sexual insults, arousing our deepest fears about men and about the Internet (pornography, secrecy, debasement of women, possible violence). When boys have done something so scary, so obviously wrong, it is difficult to go to the administrators at the school and say, "You know, these boys have been mightily provoked by the girls." Isn't that blaming the victim? We've all been taught that you must not do that; that's what slimy lawyers used to try to do in rape cases. How are you going to argue that the girls "deserved it" because of what they said to the boys? That's a tough and risky position to take in our culture.

Still, I believe that boys must be defended at times like these. They are, after all, just seventh graders. Their judgment was bad, but they were provoked, and no one had stopped the girls from preying on them. You must go to your school administrators and say, "If you punish just these boys, it is an injustice. They have made a mistake, yet we must understand their suffering." It is an unpopular position, and most administrators will greet it with fear. How can they not punish sexual harassment?

Still, if we want boys to behave morally in school—and later in life—we must show them even-handed justice in school. I have never been in a school where girl crimes were spotted as quickly or punished as severely as boy crimes. Most boys accept that inequity in a good-natured way. After all, boys do take more obvious pleasure in tweaking authority than girls do. But in a case such as the one you describe, the boys will grow bitter and angry if no one stands up for them.

Many men are reluctant to stand up for boys. Indeed, adult men also accept that there is no way to argue effectively against a charge of sexual harassment. So they advise boys, "You just can't do that," and they expect the boys to take their punishment. A situation like this requires a woman to stand up and say, "This is unfair. These girls were mean." Only a woman has the credibility to make that statement and make it stick.

Cracking the Code of Silence

Q: *I have been trying to crack down on bullying and cruelty in the school where I serve as vice principal. One of my biggest obstacles is the wall of silence. Even the victims of the worst* *cruelty won't tell on the perpetrators, or else they will report an incident and then retract it later, making it impossible for me to follow through effectively with the bully or his parents. Is there anything I can do?*

A: I have a lot of empathy for you—you wish to intervene to stop social cruelty but feel like your hands are tied. I also have a lot of empathy for the victims of violence or cruelty, who recant their reports out of fear of reprisals or out of misguided loyalty to the group and to the code of silence. You face a tough problem, or really, three tough problems. First, how can you get victims to report cruelty so that something can be done to respond and to prevent further incidents? Second, how can you help the children who are being cruel to take responsibility, make amends, and change their behavior if you are not able to confront them with specific allegations? And finally, how can school administrators effectively deal with teasing and bullying in the face of this wall of silence?

Studies of teasing and bullying have found that depression is the main mental health risk for those who are on the receiving end of ongoing victimization by bullies in school. Fortunately, most of this depression clears up spontaneously as children grow up and social dynamics change. But for a few victims, the effects can be lifelong or can lead to an early death from suicide or risk-taking behaviors. But why is depression the most common negative consequence of being bullied? Why not posttraumatic stress disorder, phobias, anxiety attacks, or some other symptom of mental illness? I think depression is the most typical result because being teased and bullying isn't just a matter of being humiliated or beaten up or scared. The rules of group life say that you can't even speak up about what you have experienced, and that makes it even worse. Depression is our mind's response to serious traumas that we can't get over because we can't speak out about them or talk them through.

Why do children who are rejected or brutalized, whether by a single bully or by the whole class, still follow that group rule of silence? Why don't they reject those rules and abandon the group, as they have been rejected and abandoned? The answer is painfully simple. We are social creatures, and we can literally die if we are not part of the group. Even if we don't actually die, it can feel as if we are going to.

Let's look at our cousins, the apes and monkeys, who are also social animals. Adolescent male baboons, for example, all have to leave their home troop to make a go of it in a new troop. For up to a month they sit on the outskirts of this new group, hoping to be accepted. They try picking fights to prove their fighting ability, a skill the new group might find useful. They try looking invisible so they can blend in with the crowd. Not every baboon makes it into a new group during this difficult period, and they aren't always welcomed back into their old troop. Among a group of monkeys on a little island off Puerto Rico, the situation for adolescent males is even worse. As many as 20 to 25 percent of them don't live through this mandatory initiation into a new group. Those that are finally accepted are not likely to do anything that will jeopardize their position as a member of the group.

Do those primate scenes sound familiar? We simply have to be part of a group. Of course, some children seem to feel this need more strongly than others do, and for them, the threat of rejection and exclusion is even more painful and intolerable. But everyone feels it to some extent. Among groups of children from age eight to twenty, breaking the code of silence—being a "rat"—is the one sure way to be completely rejected by a group. This is a powerful rule. At some military academies, newcomers are beaten just to see if they will tell; only if they don't are they then exposed to systematic hazing. We think these facts of group life explain why victims of cruelty so often keep the code of silence, or if they do report abuse, why they often will later change their story to protect the guilty parties. It is bad enough to be on the outskirts of a group, teased or bullied without any support or help from the so-called innocent bystanders. But ostracism, complete isolation from the group, is much, much worse—and that's what children face if they turn someone in or get someone in trouble.

The force of this rule is so strong that even people who oppose the original teasing and (theoretically) support the rights of the victim to be safe will usually join forces with the bullies to form a united front against the whistle-blower. At one high school a boy reluctantly reported a friend and classmate for smoking marijuana, hoping to get the boy some help with his drug problem. Absolutely everyone in the class turned on the whistle-blower, including some friends who had never even liked the boy he had turned in. The punishment that he withstood for the next few months was intense. It wasn't that the other students didn't believe him when he insisted he was just trying to get help for someone he considered a friend. It's just that those kinds of considerations don't matter when such a basic group rule is violated.

Another way to look at this overarching need to be in a group is from the perspective of roles. Every group hands out roles to its members. Some people are leaders, some are followers, some are on the fringe, and so on. And the role of the victim is often preferable to the role of the rat or stool pigeon, because a victim remains a member of the group—a despised member of the group, certainly, but still within the circle. But a complete outsider has no group, and that's the risk faced by a whistle-blower. As bad as it can be to be a victim, the worst punishments dished out by groups are reserved for people who break the code of silence. They are seen as betraying the integrity and even the very existence of the group.

When faced with well-known but unreported abuses or with recanted testimony, school administrators often find themselves exhorting the victims to spill the beans. We hate to see kids shoot themselves in the foot by protecting others who would not go out of their way to protect them. But it's much more effective to take those students who are known victims, or seem likely to be victims, and teach them assertiveness and social skills so that they can do a better job of standing up for themselves. That doesn't mean we throw them to the lions. We still commit ourselves to making the school a safe place for everyone, but we do this by helping everyone be a valued member of the group rather than by fighting a losing battle against the code of silence.

This dynamic of groups does not happen only among children and teenagers. Adults are just as bad. Look at what we do to whistle-blowers. We hang them out to dry, even if we recognize the courage it takes to blow the whistle on a powerful group that is doing something we agree is morally wrong. Many militant groups reserve their worst vengeance not for the declared enemy but for those from their own group who are considered turncoats or informers.

The first thing schools have to understand is how primal is that need to protect the group, even a group that mistreats you. Next, schools need to help bullies and other perpetrators of social cruelty take responsibility for their behavior and change it.

I spent a few years working as a psychologist with criminals, who taught me more than I ever wanted to know about evading responsibility. A common problem in the prosecution of criminals and in the psychological treatment of criminals is that victims often recant their testimony because they are afraid of or intimidated by the perpetrator. That leaves the offender with no incentive to take responsibility for himself or to change, and it leaves the prosecutor in a tough spot. When our goal is punishment, we require proof and consistent testimony. But my job as a therapist was not to find a verdict or to punish. My colleagues and I had the goal of helping criminals change their thinking and their behavior, to take responsibility, to make amends to their victims, and to maintain a new way of living in the world as members of the group, not as predators. So we weren't as dependent on the facts of each case as prosecutors have to be. That allowed us to explore deeper issues with the perpetrators, about who they were and how they wanted to live their lives. We talked about how they came across to others as opposed to how they viewed themselves. Our tactic was to say that *all* allegations of criminal or abusive behavior signal a problem, even if the victim later changed his story out of fear. I won't say that the work was quick or easy, or even that it was successful more than half the time. And I don't want to compare the average school bully with a hardened criminal. But I mention it because I think the answer to the code of silence is to move away from punishment as the school's response, and instead to take a more psychological and behavioral approach. This isn't being "soft" on teasing and bullying; it is being effective. Neither the bully nor the victim is willing to settle things by simply reporting abuses and punishing the wrongdoers. A more subtle approach is needed.

One tactic that doesn't require rock-solid evidence is to say to suspected bullies, "Whenever people talk about teasing and bullying around here, your name always comes up." Another tactic is to increase supervision so that eyewitness reports can come from staff instead of only from victims, who face such pressure to keep quiet. We can even soft-sell this supervision to the bully: "You know that when something happens everyone looks at you. If you are being wrongly accused, then we have to keep a close eye on things for your protection."

We need to go beyond a punishment approach so that we can find out what motivates cruel behavior on the part of students. Some kids feel like outsiders and strike out in revenge against the world or against individual students they resent, and others feel like they are on the top of the heap and think the regular rules don't apply to them or that they are just "telling it like it is" when they torment a lower-status child. Obviously, the response in these two types of situations needs to be completely different, even though the cruel behavior may be quite similar. Bullies who feel like outsiders have to be brought into the circle of inclusion and respect that defines a good group. Bullies who are abusing their power as leaders have to be taught win-win strategies and other aspects of good leadership. Of course, both types of bullies need help with empathy and responsibility.

Too Thin

Q: *I got a sinking feeling in my stomach the other day when my daughter told me that most of the girls in her fourth-grade class were on a diet. I didn't expect this so soon. As of now, my daughter is saying that she thinks it's "silly" and has no intention of being on a diet—but I suspect that she'll feel pressured soon to follow along with the crowd. Is there anything I can do to help protect my perfectly normal-sized daughter from thinking that she's too fat or that being overweight is the worst thing in the world? Is there anything I can do to help the other girls?*

A: Many parents are surprised that young girls become obsessed with weight—but recent studies about anorexia show that girls as young as age eight are dieting and are at risk for developing the destructive eating disorder. Younger and younger girls are exposed to a media saturation of "perfect" bodies that are actually underweight to an unhealthy degree. In addition, prepubescent girls are being portrayed in magazines and on TV as sexy young women instead of girls.

Your daughter's classroom is an excellent illustration of the type of primitive Darwinism that seems to rule in junior high—or even sooner. By "primitive Darwinism" I mean that popularity and status are based on the most superficial aspects of success. The qualities of strength (for boys) and beauty (for girls) attain an inflated importance in childhood peer groups. These exaggerated ideals of femininity and masculinity determine a great deal of social ranking in every school. It is quite amazing that these traits show up on children's radar at a very young age, long before they choose partners for those all-important human mating rituals. And as we all know, these qualities continue to have exaggerated importance for grown-ups, as I realize with great anguish every year that Brad Pitt or Pierce Brosnan edges me out for sexiest man alive on the cover of *People*!

The basis for deciding who gets to be popular hasn't changed much over the years. Boys continue to be valued for traits and achievements that signal success at hunting or fighting against the neighboring cave. Girls are valued for their appearance and their sociability—indicators of their future promise for childbearing and homemaking. Popular girls and boys tend to be the most traditionally feminine or the most traditionally masculine of their peers. And the least popular kids are often the ones who stray too far from the norms for their gender. Look at who gets teased the most in school: incompetent or effeminate boys, and unattractive or aggressive girls.

For girls, the risk of this excessive focus on appearance is that they will develop eating disorders, serious distortions about their body image, or even a form of self-loathing based on not having the "right" body or looks. Anorexia can be fatal. Bulimia, which is a cycle of bingeing on food and then purging by vomiting or taking laxatives, has many serious health repercussions as well. The even more common cycle of dieting and then regaining the weight is also risky for a girl's health. And this fixation by girls on thinness and stereo-typed conceptions of beauty is indeed beginning younger and younger.

Mary Pipher, author of *Reviving Ophelia*, quotes a study about girls' self-esteem dropping dramatically within minutes of reading fashion magazines. This is not a coincidence. Critics of the advertising industry argue persuasively that most ads work by making people feel bad, and then offering them the solution to their misery: Buy this product and feel better! Even today's teenagers and preteens, as media-savvy as they are, are suckers for this multibillion-dollar marketing onslaught.

The federal government's commitment to Title IX, which guarantees girls' access to athletics, has made a huge impact on the lives of girls. They can now gain status and prestige from athletic prowess as well as from appearance and sociability. But there is still a need for role models for girls who match every type of body and who excel in every area of society—and not because of looks.

Of course, it is not just girls who face risks to their physical health and their mental health because of unrealistic and damaging notions of what they are supposed to look like and how they are supposed to behave. Boys experience pressure to "bulk up," to put on muscle mass and lift weights to a point that is dangerous, especially if they use steroids or other drugs to enhance the process. Boys also experience the harsh reality that their own interests and strengths may not be valued at all by the group. That's because the group is locked in the primitive Darwinism that sees male strength and athleticism as the be-all and end-all.

The clearest example of this I have heard recently is

from a mother in Louisiana. Her son told her that in his third-grade class, boys are picked to sit at the cool table based on how well they played football that day. He's a so-so athlete and isn't all that interested in being better at football—but he's devastated to be left out of the group. Usually boys are a little subtler about this, but the message is the same. Even when sorting based on size and athletic ability is less obvious, it is still pervasive. Just as with the girls, popularity and dominance are largely established on the basis of stereotyped gender norms. Fortunately, as boys get older, there are other ways they can excel and receive recognition from the group—or at least from a subgroup with similar interests. Skateboarding, drama, writing, academics, music—these are all ways that a child can find confidence and validation, even if the group as a whole continues to overvalue athletics, strength, and even aggression.

Many individuals and organizations are working to change this situation for girls. One of my favorites is a group called Dads and Daughters. In addition to promoting close connections between fathers and their daughters, this group is active in teaching families and schools about the risks of eating disorders and other dangerous outcomes of our national obsession with girls' appearance. On their Web site, for example, they quote a report from the BBC that only 1 percent of young women surveyed were happy with their bodies. The same survey found that 10 percent had taken drugs in an attempt to lose weight, 80 percent "thought about their body size or shape every day," and almost as many considered themselves depressed over their weight. A majority felt that thinness was the most important ingredient to success.

One of the most disturbing findings of this survey, which

brings to mind the thin girls in your daughter's class putting themselves on diets, is that most of the young women surveyed wanted to be thinner whether they were overweight or not. Those who were already underweight, based on medical norms, wanted to be even thinner. Meanwhile, the ones who were overweight all reported that they had been ostracized or humiliated by others because of their weight. The results of this one survey are fairly typical of research into body image and eating disorders among girls and young women.

Perhaps you are wondering what all of this information has to do with peer groups and friendship. Eating disorders used to be seen as an individual matter, a mental illness based on family disturbance or genetics. But the current understanding is that they are in part social problems. Bulimia, for example, can sweep through a school, affecting as many as two-thirds or more of the girls in a grade. Groups of girls can egg each other on, pressuring one another to be thinner and thinner, or ostracizing anyone who isn't keeping up. Girls who are overweight or who are a perfect size for their genetic makeup can be seen as losers, and they suffer tremendously for it. The fact that your daughter comes home and says all the fourth-grade girls are on diets makes it clear that this isn't an individual problem; it is a social issue.

That means the solution has to be social as well. In addition to the important one-on-one conversations you have with your own daughter about dieting, weight, appearance, and following the crowd, the school has to be involved as well. Parents can have PTO meetings on the topic, or sponsor parent support groups focused on talking with children about body image. Adults and children also need more media literacy. Media-savvy kids and parents can look critically at images on TV and in magazines and understand that they are being sold a bill of goods about how they are supposed to look and how they are supposed to feel about themselves if they don't look that way. Schools need to confront the primitive Darwinism head on, for example, by getting rid of the tradition that the head cheerleader and the captain of the football team are king and queen of the homecoming court. For our daughters, we have to make sure other things besides athletics and looks are valued in the school.

As parents, we have to model a healthy approach to eating and exercise and stop making comments about how cute the slender (or skinny) girls look. We can encourage girls to participate in sports, science fairs, and community service projects—anything that takes their focus off their own appearance and the appearance of their peers—to help them pay attention to something more constructive. Most of all, we can encourage our children to put their energy into friendship instead of popularity, because friends value each other for who they are inside, not how little they weigh.

Helping Children Deal with a Difficult Peer

Q: *Is it okay to talk to my class about a socially inept kid, with the kid absent? All my students are uncomfortable with Hayley, but I think that they just need a little guidance in how to handle her. I am afraid, though, that it could just cement the idea that she is different.*

A: This is a tough question to answer. I can imagine a gifted teacher successfully pulling off something like this—but I can also imagine such a talk backfiring. It sounds like you have a pretty good feeling that the class just needs a little gentle push in the right direction. But you are worried that calling attention to the problem would give the impression that you are endorsing the idea that Hayley is different from everyone else.

It can be hard to balance the potential risks against the potential benefits of this type of intervention. I wish I could resolve your dilemma with a simple red light or green light, but I'm afraid I can't. The best approach depends so much on your personality and your teaching style, and also on the dynamics of your particular classroom and the nature of Hayley's social difficulties. So instead of giving you a yes-or-no answer, I'd like to step back and look at two broader issues implied by your question: How direct or indirect should an intervention be? And who should receive the intervention (the target child alone, the whole class, or the rest of the class with the target child absent)?

A completely direct approach would be to say to the class something along these lines: "People in this classroom are being really mean to Hayley and I want it to stop." "You all need to understand that Hayley is different, and I expect you to be tolerant and accepting of those differences." "I've noticed that some people in the class have some questions about how to be a good friend to Hayley. What can we all do to help Hayley feel more welcome and included in our class?" Another direct approach is to bring up several recent examples and problem-solve with the class how to handle those conflicts more effectively.

You will notice immediately that these examples of direct interventions are quite varied in their tone and their focus, but they all confront the key issues head on. The advantage of addressing the problem directly is that everything is out on the table. Children often perceive teachers as not knowing or not caring about their social problems, so a direct approach makes it clear that you do know and you do care.

The potential problem with a direct approach is that it can put rejected children on the spot, or set them up for further rejection. If the targeted child is present during the discussion, everyone may stare or say mean things under the guise of "helping." If she isn't there, she might be targeted later for "getting the class in trouble" or for being the teacher's pet.

I don't mean to scare anyone away from a direct approach, which is often the fastest and most effective way to handle a social problem in the classroom. But I do want to raise awareness about the potential hazards to consider carefully before diving in. You're wondering whether a direct approach might cement the idea that this girl is different. In my experience, that's not usually one of the hazards that we have to worry about. If *you* are aware of the difference, then you can be sure that the children are aware of it too. We want to protect vulnerable children from humiliation, but they face humiliation every day. Sometimes the child would prefer to have it addressed directly. He or she will respond by feeling protected and cared about, rather than singled out and "hung out to dry."

A slightly less direct approach might be "I have noticed

that the class has been having a lot of difficulty in getting along. Has anyone else noticed that?" or "I'd like us to review as a class how we've been doing lately in following our basic guidelines of respecting one another and making an extra effort to include everyone in activities." These intermediate approaches let children be in charge of framing the problem and the solutions. Hayley might surprise you by speaking up for herself—but she gets to choose. Or an unexpected ally might emerge as Trish says, "Yeah, people are mean to Hayley sometimes and I don't know how to get them to stop."

An indirect solution would be to show a film that includes themes or situations similar to what you have been observing in the classroom. Then, during the class discussion afterward, the children can decide how much to personalize it. When I lead discussions with kids after a movie, I am always reluctant to ask directly if anyone can relate to the more painful aspects of what we've just watched. But inevitably, a few minutes into the discussion, some brave soul will raise a hand and talk about his or her own experience. Often that happens after a few students insist that "nothing like that could happen here in our school." The showing of a film and the openness of the discussion allow the more marginal students to speak out and say that yes, there is racism here; yes, there are cliques here; yes, people are teased for being slower readers, for having less money, for being a different religion. A good discussion like this, which allows children to decide for themselves whether they want to talk about themselves or about the characters in the film, can also provide a safe environment for revealing acts of kindness and compassion. A new student might say that she felt like a complete outsider and cried into her pillow every night until someone came over and made friends with her one day.

Some other indirect approaches are to find that one rejected child's strength and create an opportunity for him or her to shine in front of the class, or to devote class time to a big project that requires everyone to cooperate and take on a vital role.

Some approaches are in the border zone between direct and indirect. One such strategy is to have regularly scheduled class meetings about social issues. Special meetings, called to address a particular problem, are often emotionally loaded. Therefore many teachers have found that it works better to have regular meetings once or twice a week, where social issues can be discussed. That way it becomes routine and consistent, and a sense of safety is built up that can be called upon when a more serious issue arises. Regular meetings can also prevent many difficulties from escalating out of control. At any particular meeting the teacher (and students) can decide whether to raise particular issues directly ("Hayley always grabs everyone's stuff") or indirectly ("Let's all take three deep breaths so we can relax and focus better").

In deciding whether to use a direct or an indirect approach, it is important to consider just what the children in the class need. If they simply need a little basic information about a certain child's physical or emotional condition, then it may be helpful for you, or the child's parent, to talk directly to the rest of the class and answer questions. On the other hand, if the children are in need of a higher dose of kindness and compassion, if they understand all too well why that particular child is annoying or different and are unkind about it, then a direct approach may not work.

The next question to consider is who will be the recipient of your direct or indirect intervention. As you suggest in your question, the most important aspect of this is whether the child in question should be present or absent. The first step in making this decision, often forgotten by teachers, is to talk it over with the child and her parents. We often jump to the conclusion that a child would be mortified to be in the room during a discussion of her behavior and how it affects the rest of the class. But some children wouldn't mind that at all, and instead are mortified by the idea that the class would be talking about her behind her back. I think it's important to reassure the child and the parents that either way, present or absent, you will do your best to keep the discussion respectful and thoughtful, but that you can't guarantee that people won't say anything that hurts her feelings.

I don't blame teachers for assuming such discussions are best done with the target child absent. Teachers are generally empathic to the suffering of the child who is singled out or different or disliked. When the teacher brings up the behavior of a particularly difficult child, the rest of the class may need a chance to vent their feelings of anger or annoyance and resentment about that child. That kind of venting might be necessary for the class to work through those feelings, to make friends across the lines of difference, and to become a cohesive group. But it might be too painful for the child to listen to those negative feelings. On the other hand, if the child is absent, there is a danger that the rest of the class will take the discussion as an opportunity to compile a laundry list of resentments and complaints and criticisms, outdoing each other in attacking the child. As the teacher and the facilitator of the discussion, you have to protect her from that kind of escalation even if she is not in the room.

Talking to the whole class or to the class minus one are not the only options available. In some situations the best intervention is to have a one-on-one talk with a classroom leader. This might be a ringleader of the teasing and excluding, whom you can prevail upon to stop behaving that way. Or it could be a prosocial leader, whom you can ask to take the difficult child under his or her wing and lead the way in changing the classroom dynamics.

Another place to target your intervention might be right in the middle of a difficult interaction, with the two or three children involved. This has the advantage of being rooted in immediate details rather than in generalities about one child's personality or limitations. For example, let's say Hayley grabs Ted's pencil out of his hand, and Ted shoves her and yells at her. That can be a teachable moment, allowing you to sit down with the two of them and ask each one what they could have done differently.

Of course, often you will choose to work directly with the targeted child on improving her social skills. But even if the primary intervention is with one particular child, it may still be necessary to talk things over with the class as a whole. Systems don't like to change, and a child who has been pegged as socially inept may retain that label even after she learns effective social skills. The system needs a new script, a new story about itself. For example: "We used to be divided and now we are united." "We used to not understand or celebrate our differences, but now we appreciate everyone for their special strengths." Or (perhaps more honestly) "We used to think Hayley was a pain in the neck or a poor misunderstood victim, but now she's changed and we've changed, so all together we are proud to be Mrs. Musser's class."

Coming to the Rescue

Q: *I teach in a learning differences program, and there is an eighth-grade boy named Robert who is overweight, does not speak very well, and is very clumsy. The other boys treat him so badly. They call him names, leave mean messages on his phone, and so on. Robert is constantly trying to stick up for himself, but it just seems to make things worse. How do I deal with this situation? How do I work with the kids who are teasing him and also help Robert realize what he can do to help his situation?*

A: Robert must feel like he is the last defender of the Alamo. It sounds as if he is completely alone. Does he have no friends at all? Are there any kids who will stand up for him, or at least leave him alone? Though he is courageous, he will soon become psychologically overwhelmed unless reinforcements arrive—and the reinforcements in this case must be the adults. Teachers and parents must make clear to the other children that they are not going to be allowed to torture Robert for their own amusement.

It is not going to be easy, because the children have become accustomed to tormenting him. In fact, that activity is part of what makes them feel okay about themselves and their own learning troubles. It is also part of what holds them together as a group. They will experience the teachers as attacking their autonomy and will resist the adults who try to help Robert. You and the other teachers are going to have to make a concerted effort over time to make the learning differences program a more tolerant environment. I will get to the practical aspects of that in a minute. First I would like to say something about the downside of special programs for children, even though I believe in them strongly.

Programs for children with learning differences can sometimes be hazardous places, because all of the children in them have experienced some failure in mainstream classrooms. All of the children are "different" in some way, and all of them undoubtedly wish that they were just "normal." In an ideal world, putting all the children with learning difficulties together in one learning center should create an environment of acceptance. Unfortunately, often it does not. Life does not usually turn out like *The Mighty Ducks* or *The Bad News Bears*, in which a group of outcast kids, all losers by some conventional definition, come together and find their strengths under the guidance of a kindly coach. Children with learning disabilities or children who are overweight have been teased since they first came to school. Almost without exception, they have been excluded from the most popular group or had to listen to denigrating comments. As a result, their ability to trust in other children has been corroded. They cannot imagine an environment where they could feel completely safe. So what the majority do is create an environment where they, at least, are on the strong side of the teasing. If they can find one child who is unmistakably different, they all go after him, shaming him and pointing out his differences: "He's not like us! He's fat! He's the loser!"

The subtext is, "Not us!" All of a sudden the children doing the teasing are in charge of what is mainstream. No matter how different the children in your program are compared to students in regular classrooms, if they can find a scapegoat onto whom they can project all of their inadequacies, they feel better.

This process is human. It operates to a small extent in all human groups, though rarely does it focus so exclusively on one child. In your classroom, however, you face a particularly tough problem. Robert provides the other children with three reasons to attack him. He is overweight, he is clumsy, and he speaks poorly. The first taps into a prejudice that is almost universal in this country; the second taps into one of the biggest fears of eighth-grade boys, that of not being athletic; the third makes him sound babyish to other kids. That is a lot to overcome.

It would help if he were in a classroom with other children who had multiple difficulties, but I imagine that you have thought of that and there is no other alternative for Robert. As long as Robert is there, you have to work to create a culture of tolerance for him. The first step would be to talk to Robert's parents about what you are trying to achieve and ask for their support. If you tell the parents of the other eighth-grade boys that their sons are ganging up on one child, they will know instantly that you are talking about Robert. They have listened to their boys heap abuse on Robert in car rides home from school. They just haven't known what to do about it. You need to ask for the moral support of those parents for your efforts.

Second, you need to define your classroom as a place that is a safe place for difference. Gently, persistently, and daily, you have to remind your students that they are in a learning *differences* program. Everyone in the classroom is different. That's how they got there. Remind them that no one likes being different in eighth grade. I would recommend that you show a film about a group of middle-school children and an excluded child, particularly an overweight one. Such characters feature in both movies I mentioned earlier, *The Mighty Ducks* and *The Bad News Bears*. This is a visual generation raised on movies. Nothing will get to them as effectively as seeing the pain of an overweight boy portrayed on the screen. Have a discussion about the movie. Ask about the pain of the fat boy in the film. Perhaps Robert will have the courage to speak up in class and identify himself with that boy.

In time, it will be important for Robert to be in a weight-loss program and to get speech therapy and occupational therapy for his clumsiness. It would also help if he was in a social skills group, often called "friendship groups" in schools. The weight loss and speech improvement, however, are long-term goals. In the short term he needs to be protected. You cannot expect him to have the skills to work his way out of his situation on his own. No one in eighth grade has the social skills to get out of the scapegoat role. Robert needs your help, and he needs it now.

Removing the Kick Me Sign

Q: *My son is tortured at school, and it makes him miserable. Whenever I complain to the school or to other parents, they suggest that it's because he is awkward or different. Well,*

*everyone's different, and that doesn't excuse the other kids
from being mean and cruel. How do I get the school, the bullies, and their parents to accept responsibility and stop treat-
ing my son like it's his fault he gets picked on?*

A: Our schools and our society do need to take a stronger
stand on protecting children. No one deserves to be teased
and bullied, especially if they are being singled out for mistreatment because of some difference in their appearance,
personality, or learning style. I can understand why it feels
like "blaming the victim" when people at the school or other
parents change the subject from your son's victimization to
his own difficulties with social skills. On the other hand, if
your child does have social skills deficits (that's the fancy
way of saying he has trouble making and keeping friends or
being part of a group), then he does need a hand with those
skills or else he'll always be out of step. (See page 48 for
more details on social skills.) You don't give all the details,
but I am assuming that if everyone tells you that your son is
awkward and a little odd, then there probably is some truth
to that. Of course, that doesn't justify his being tortured in
any way, but it might help explain it.

So you're right that it isn't fair that the burden should be
on your son to change just so he won't be targeted with
meanness and cruelty. Being safe should be every child's
birthright. But the others are right too, because on a practical level it often makes sense to focus on helping a child to
develop the skills they lack in order to be well accepted and
well liked.

In other words, focusing on social skills does not automatically mean that someone is blaming the victim. Instead,

I like to think of social skills training as removing the invisible Kick Me sign that some children seem to wear.

Were you ever the victim of that practical joke where the other kids secretly tape a sign that says Kick Me onto someone's back? The "joke" is that it takes a while to figure out why people are kicking you, pointing at you, and laughing. I don't think anyone has ever made a scientific study of this practical joke, but even without a research grant, I think we can guess what such a study would find. I would predict that about a third of kids will kick the child if they see a Kick Me sign. Another third will laugh when the kid is kicked, and most of the rest will do nothing. That leaves precious few who will go over and take the sign off to end the "game."

In a way, that imaginary experiment points the way to what is needed to address social cruelty. We have to step in with every one of these groups. We need to teach the kickers to be less cruel, the victims to wise up, and the bystanders to be more involved. We need to teach everyone to go out of their way to be more compassionate and helpful—to remove the Kick Me signs from others' backs.

Some children seem to invite abuse from their peers in subtle and not-so-subtle ways. Of course, step one is always to stop the abuse, intervening with the cruel and aggressive children. But we also have to step in and help the child being abused to be a good friend and a full-fledged member of the group—and that means social skills training.

Perhaps it isn't fair that the child who has been singled out for rejection is singled out once again to have to learn how to *not* be a target. But fairness is really beside the point. The point is for the child to have friendships and a sense of belonging in the group, and that requires an understanding of the basis for the teasing or exclusion. Some children are targeted at random, or because of being new to the school, or because of physical characteristics such as skin color, weight, or size. But some children are targeted because of how they behave, especially how they interact with their peers. Does that justify cruelty? Absolutely not. Is it fair? Probably not. Does it need to be addressed as part of the solution? Absolutely yes. We can't just exhort children not to kick the kid who is wearing a Kick Me sign. We also have to help him reach around and take that sign off.

I met with some parents of fourth graders recently and heard this story about a boy who had trouble fitting in. He had always been a little different from the other kids, academically smart but socially awkward. He had a few friends but was teased a lot, especially by the most athletic boys. The last straw was a note in his desk from an anonymous boy (though the teacher and some of the other parents thought they knew who it was from). The note said, "Dear asshole, you had better stop wearing those prep clothes." A couple of boys had previously teased him about his rather old-fashioned clothes.

The teacher handled the situation well, according to his mother and several other parents who were involved. For one thing, the teacher said that she had found the note in his desk, so it wouldn't look like he had reported it. At our parent meeting, the mother wanted to know if she should buy him new clothes. Would that give the message that he caved in to the teasing and abuse? Or would that protect him from more abuse, even though it meant that the other kids won? The other parents in the meeting had a wide range of advice for this mom. A few commented that they had noticed that he did tend to wear too-adult clothes—including ties—that set him apart from the others, and he should be counseled gently not to wear them anymore. Some were ready to rush in and clobber the suspected perpetrators of the mean teasing.

It's a tricky situation, isn't it? We don't want to buy into the idea that everyone has to be exactly the same. But we also need to help out children who are not good at noticing or participating in the group norms, like how to dress and how to talk and how to act. It's one thing when an older child deliberately decides to reject these norms, understanding the social consequences. But when younger children are unable to follow them and can't understand why they are rejected, then we need to step in and help them fit in. And we also need to try to stop the mean-spirited enforcement of those arbitrary rules. If we work on both sides of this at once, we can have the biggest impact on the kick-me/kick-you dynamics in a classroom.

No One Is Safe Unless Everyone Is Safe

Q: *How can we get the majority of parents in a school, whose children are doing fine socially, to care about the children who are suffering or struggling? Whenever I try to talk to other parents about social issues, all I hear is that we have to focus on "the basics" and test scores. I guess kindness and compassion don't improve test scores.*

A: My one-word answer is this: Columbine. I think the terrible shootings at Columbine High School, and other high-profile school killings, have revealed to all of us that the social climate of a school affects everyone, at every level. We can't just hide our heads in the sand and say that the children who are at the top of the social hierarchy, or those solidly in the middle, have nothing to worry about. We can't just ignore the neglected and rejected children, or try to identify and punish a few bullies, and think we have tackled the problems that confront our schools.

In response to those tragic school-related deaths, we are forced to confront over and over again the dynamics of rejected children who snap under pressure and react with violence. This violent reaction is often an escalation—an extreme escalation—of mistreatment they experienced themselves at the hands of the group. The violence is usually not committed by a "crazy person" out of the blue. It is usually a statement about what the perpetrator perceives as an intolerable social situation. Recognizing this in no way diminishes the magnitude of the crime or the responsibility of the criminal, but it makes us realize that the fallout from these social flash points affects every child at a school, and all of their families.

We would like to be able to prevent school violence by predicting which students are likely to be the perpetrators. That way we could just take care of those few students and no one else would have to worry about the deeper social forces at work. But identifying future violent offenses is not an easy task. In fact, it may be impossible. We might also like to improve school security with metal detectors and bomb-sniffing dogs, but those may not be the best answers either.

As hard as psychologists and law enforcement agencies have tried to draw up a profile of a school-age killer, it is simply not possible to identify every potentially violent person. We can suspend or expel every child who makes a threat, writes a violent poem, or listens to certain bands, but we'd have to empty our schools. Most of those children are not at higher risk for being violent than anyone else is.

School violence occurs in a social context. There is often a history of escalating conflicts, rejection by peers, anti-social friends or groups egging one another on, relationship breakups, and adult detachment. The constantly changing nature of this background makes it hard to pinpoint exactly who is at risk for being violent and when. A potentially dangerous situation may be averted by a caring interaction with a teacher or a peer, and we never know how close we came to tragedy. On the other hand, a student might be considered a very low risk, but a chain of events could quickly push him or her over the edge.

If we can't identify those who are likely to become violent, what *can* we do? We can create a culture in the school that promotes acceptance and inclusion, does not tolerate rejection or neglect, and focuses on the responsibility of bystanders to take a stand against all forms of bullying and meanness. We also need smaller, more caring schools, places where every child is greeted by an adult who knows his or her name, makes eye contact, shakes a hand, and checks in if something seems to be amiss.

Since social dynamics are fluid, the adults in a school have to know children well in order to make ongoing assessments of risk, as opposed to trying to pick out the "bad apples" and get rid of them. Effective prevention of violence also requires a shift in priorities away from punishment and detection and toward community and connection. Knowing children, and having warm and supportive relationships with them, provides better security in a school than metal detectors or armed guards. And it works. In a recent incident in Massachusetts, still pending in the judicial system, it appears that a close relationship between a student and a teacher may have prevented a Columbine-style massacre.

Why should everyone care about the few children who are suffering socially? From a moral perspective, the answer is clear. Dr. Martin Luther King Jr. said that no one is free unless everyone is free. We can paraphrase this high ideal to say that no one is truly safe in a school unless everyone is safe.

3

AT SCHOOL AND IN THE NEIGHBORHOOD: *The Social World of Children*

Whenever children gather, they immediately begin to conduct experiments with love, identity, power, and social cruelty. Do they know they are conducting experiments? Of course not! They would say they're just being kids. Nevertheless, anyone can see that they are testing each other all the time. Look at how brothers and sisters push each other's buttons at dinner—their "experiments" ask the eternal question "How much needling will it take to make him blow up or cry?" Add in some cousins or a few kids from the neighborhood and the teasing and social interplay become that much more complex: older against younger, girls against boys, the school-haters against the school-lovers.

Children make bold public moves that ask the question "If I try to be boss, will anyone follow my lead?" These experiments are difficult to understand at times, because many of them are high risk and they're being conducted simultaneously. You wouldn't want to try that in a biology lab! But if you watch any group of children for an extended period of time you will see the whole human condition on display: kindness and cruelty, loyalty and treachery, intimacy and isolation. The dance of affection and aggression that characterizes human life is spontaneously and intricately choreographed and played out among children every minute they are together.

Where can you go to see young people conducting their experiments and dancing their dances? Schools, of course. Look in the halls during breaks; observe cafeterias, locker rooms, bathrooms, and classrooms. That is where children spend so much of their young lives. Classrooms are laboratories designed for children's social experimentation. All the "equipment" is there: a group of children of different ages, races, abilities, and economic backgrounds. Everyone is in intimate contact with one another for hours each day, week after week, for years.

We are social animals, highly dependent upon others for our safety, survival, and comfort. There is an almost insatiable individual human need for company, for touch, and for reassuring conversation. When we visit an all-girls school and get a chance to meet with the students in an informal setting, they sit close together, lie in their friends' laps, and play with each other's hair. Boys are not so openly affectionate, but they often sit close and play bumping, shoving games. Boys too need contact. Yet alongside this comforting physical presence provided by other kids, a psychological tension builds because there is also a profound human need for status in a group.

Children are always looking for connection, but they are also seeking recognition and power. Many times these drives are mutually exclusive. It is, for example, hard to keep a warm connection with a friend when she is trying to force you to recognize how important and knowledgeable she is. If you're watching the movie *Harry Potter and the Sorcerer's Stone* with a friend who has already seen it, and she insists on telling you everything that is going to happen, it can be mightily irritating (it certainly is for the adults in the row behind you). But for the most part, your shared friendship—not to mention your capacity for forgiveness—overrides such transitory moments of know-it-all bossiness.

However, the tensions among three human drives—for connection, for recognition, and for power—mean that whenever people are together there will be conflict. That's how it is at school, at camp, or in the neighborhood. Whenever and wherever children gather, conflict will arise sooner or later.

A complex set of invisible rules governs the behavior of children when they are together. The first rule is well known: Children must be like their peers. The tendency to conform starts very early. Three- or four-year-olds often express the wish to do everything their friends are doing and have the same toys their friends possess. The impulse to be the same continues until around age seven, when it starts to become even more intense. A second-grade teacher told me that she often asks children in her class to compliment each other. Very often the first boy will turn to his buddy and say, "He's cool." Once he has done that, no other boy in the class can give any compliment except "cool." If the teacher encourages one boy to branch out with a new word, he looks uncomfortable. Everyone else so far, at least all the boys, has said "cool." How can one boy break ranks and use some inferior, unmasculine word? He cannot. The invisible pressure to be like everyone else is enormous.

Most parents become quite irritated by this tendency in their kids, especially adolescents, because it feels like a conspiracy against parents. Their children are desperate to have the same clothes as their peers; they act as if they are going to die if they don't get the right cool shoes. We've all known children who have lived in dread of going to school with the "wrong" clothes on. Parents are appalled to discover that their children do not seem to have internalized any of their values. It feels as if the group teaches children to disrespect their parents.

Kids disqualify their parents from the world of their peers. At about age ten or eleven, they begin to fear that you might do something quirky in public. In answer to the question "Why don't you want your parents to help you with your social lives?" one boy said, "Because they're so old. They were born in a different time. They don't know anything about kids today." It might sound disrespectful, but this seventh-grader was simply stating that children need to learn from one another what makes you acceptable to the group. The group is *now*. It is just forming and growing. How could someone who was in seventh grade thirty years ago (which might as well have been three hundred years ago) possibly have anything helpful to say about what is acceptable to seventh graders today?

Once you start observing the pressures on children to conform to group practice you start to see the manifestations of these forces everywhere. Peer pressure—covert, subtle, and omnipresent—hovers over the head of every middle-school student. And it is clear that the pressures require sacrifice from almost every child. Children give up things they love because the group doesn't approve of them; they hide their special toys, their feelings, and their moral objections because those things don't play well with the "crowd."

The second rule of group life is that you must be a member of an identifiable group—an "us" with whom you can face all of "them." Is it inevitable that there will always be an "us" and a "them"? Can't a group of human beings like one another without excluding someone else? It is not absolutely inevitable, but the moment children begin to define the characteristics of their group ("We love N'Sync") someone outside will be perceived as not being sufficiently zealous ("She likes Blink 182 better than N'Sync"). That nonbeliever will have to be excluded from the group's inner circle because she's not quite like "us" ("She doesn't like N'Sync as much as we do"). Though it dismays us when we see children exclude one another on the basis of such trivial distinctions, it must be acknowledged that adults, not children, are the masters of the "us" and "them." We teach children how to discriminate every day. By defining people by their skin color, ethnic background, intelligence, sexual preference, geographic origin, or religious beliefs, we show children how to perceive the world through the lens of an "us" and a "them."

The third rule is that you must be "in" with the group you have chosen, or you are at risk for being "out." Once a popular group develops in eighth grade, it is likely that an "antipopular" group will soon develop—an out-group to counter the in-group. It's so painful for kids to be on the outside alone, it is so difficult not to have a tribe around them, that even low-status kids will develop into a loose coalition that can stand in opposition to the power of the popular kids. Every high school has its popular crowd and its antipopular groups. In some high schools the antipopular group may be called "Goths"; in middle schools they may be called "geeks and freaks" or the "goof troop." None of these names conveys much status. But the important thing is to join a group and feel "in" with the one with which you are identified, even if the whole group is low-status.

The last two rules of group life are that you have to find and accept your place in the social hierarchy and that you have to find and accept the role that the kids assign to you. All kids are given a place in the popularity rankings at school or in the neighborhood. That is just the way it is, and most kids are able to make their peace with the rung to which they are assigned.

Social psychology classes in college are often run on an experiential basis. The class is broken into groups that meet in a semistructured environment. Soon each group takes on a life of its own. Status and roles develop as some students become leaders, others clowns, and others critics of the process. Finally the professors allow the groups to compare notes about their group development—and to read the research on group formation. Everyone is amazed that even though the groups were randomly assigned, the same types of roles have emerged in every group, and the roles were accurately predicted by the theoretical literature. Every group has a leader and a clown; every group has an alienated outsider. Why? Group life seems to require that people fill different roles in order to balance the dynamics of the group. The rules of group life make participation in a community more coherent and predictable.

No school is without bad feeling between certain cliques. Teasing, bullying, and rejection are seen in all societies around the globe. But most of the time children solve their social problems on their own. Most of the time we can trust that peacemakers will arise among the children, that creative solutions will be found, that potential tragedies will be averted and everyone will move on.

Adults do not need to play a role in the vast majority of school and neighborhood problems. But in some situations the social dynamic runs away with the children. It is as if the experiments they are conducting suddenly blow up in their faces or produce a Frankenstein monster. Because it's a group experiment—or, rather, a number of simultaneous experiments—no one is individually responsible for it. Yet a situation arises that is destructive to the learning process for all children or traumatic for some individuals.

So what should adults do? Schools periodically encounter a "bad class," a group of apparently normal and ordinary kids who, when they are together, create chaos and bad feeling or cruelly reject low-status members. Everyone suffers as a result—both teachers and students, not to mention the learning process. Traditionally educators have tried to identify and punish the ringleaders of such a class. This strategy rarely works because it is too simplistic. The problem is bigger than any individual. It is systemic. It is in the dynamic of the group itself.

But telling a class that it is "bad" and exhorting its members to be better almost never works either. The kids feel devalued and organize against the adults, whom they perceive as critical. But they don't know how to heal themselves. The challenge for adults is to understand the complexities of the children's social organization, to enlist them as consultants in finding a solution for their destructive dynamic, and to provide them with a safe and moral framework for understanding their own struggles. It is never easy, but it is the only way to effectively solve problems that arise in schools and neighborhoods.

Adults—teachers and parents—have a responsibility to help children flourish. The cases that follow take you inside a middle school and a high school and show just how powerful and important social connection is to adolescents. The first case tells the story of how a caring adult came to the aid of isolated children and helped them find their place in the group. The second explores one of the hardest decisions a parent has to face: how to respond to teasing and exclusion that get out of hand.

CASE STUDIES

Helping Outcasts Find a Home

One night Ms. Pike thought of a ploy
That involved eleven boys
They arrived to a room full of noise
And chose the name "Baha Boyz."

The point is to discuss the problems
And help people that are in need
Anyone could come, no one stopped 'em
Ms. Pike sure did a good deed.

Fun was the only thing done
Talk about anything under the sun
The things we accomplish are greater
We all leave in a happy state.

> We can work and think like friends
> That's what makes us strong
> There's a great thing about our group
> With Baha Boyz you can't go wrong.

> *Baha Boyz rap*
> *October 2001*

The Baha Boyz love their name. One of the boys printed it out on red paper and cut the sheets into business cards—only they are business cards with a purpose. There's a line on each card that a teacher can sign to give one of the Baha Boyz permission to meet with their guidance counselor or the friendship group she started for them. The card reads:

BAHA BOYZ

student has permission to miss class

signed _____
an outstanding teacher

What teacher wouldn't want to give a boy permission to leave class if he or she received that "outstanding" designation?

One of the boys wrote a rap song giving credit for founding the Baha Boyz to Randy Pike, their guidance counselor, who has worked in that position for three decades. "The whole thirty years," she says, and then amends her own statement: "Except I taught high school for a few years in Texas." You can tell that it has been a long time since Randy has thought of herself as a teacher; at this point she is a counselor to the bone. Furthermore, she has spent the entire time talking with middle school students.

Not everyone loves middle-school kids. They can be annoying, inarticulate, disorganized, and—in the social arena—extremely cruel. Randy knows all about that. She says that the social lives of middle-schoolers are a phase. "You just have to help them get through it," she says. "You can't stop it from happening. Parents say, 'If you know it's going to happen, then stop it,' but you can't. I wish I could, but I can't."

Why are the middle grades the time of highest tension in children's social lives? Randy says, "Middle school is between when Mommy got me together with people and when I have my own means—a car."

Any middle-school teacher (or parent) knows that cliques and exclusionary behavior peak in grades six through eight, and there is always going to be a group of kids at the bottom of the popularity ladder. These low-status kids exist in every school, and they go by many different names: nerds, dorks, wonks, geeks, brainiacs, and others that we adults haven't heard yet. An engaging recent TV series about high school called them "geeks and freaks."

Randy Pike prefers not to use those names. "Last year I was able to clearly identify what I call the marginal kids, the kids who are different in some way. I invited them to have lunch with me in a conference room next to my office. I wondered what they'd think of being invited." To her surprise, they did not feel patronized by the invitation. They came with enthusiasm—and they continue to come for their weekly lunch meeting.

The Goof Troop Girls no longer call themselves by that name. These days, they're known as "The Girls." Being seventh graders, they have outgrown the name that suited them in sixth. They settled the issue in intense discussions over three lunches. "Goof Troop" was deemed too immature, and anyway it didn't fit the social ambitions of some of the girls. So they became simply The Girls.

These are not the first groups that Randy has run. She has been putting them together as long as she's been a counselor, as long as she's had the support of her principal and the faculty. She says that she can reach more kids through groups. Most children are "definitely more open" in groups than they are in individual therapy, she says. "They talk to you through another child. They know you're listening, but they say it to another child."

The secret is to make them comfortable. How does she do it? "A lot of humor," she says. "And not jumping on things they say. They say outrageous things. They're trying things out."

What do they talk about in the groups? "Friendship, how to make friends, and how to avoid being picked on," says Randy as she pulls out a pile of papers that the two groups have filled out. It's a paper-and-pencil friendship exercise. There's a line down the middle of a piece of paper, giving the kids a chance to divide their thoughts into what a good friend does and doesn't do. Under "Does" the girls have written "Helps out," "Supports you," "Does not leave you out," "Lets you have other friends," and, charmingly, "Has the name Taylor Paige."

Under the "Does Not" column the girls have written "Talk behind your back," "Leave you out," "Stalk you," and "Squirt you with squirt guns" (the last presumably a reference to boy behavior).

Randy has put up a big poster that asks What Are You Looking for in a Friend? One girl wrote, "Someone who is sporty, nice, sense of humor, common sense, acts imuture [*sic*] a lot of the time." Obviously it is important that the members of the Goof Troop—oops, I mean The Girls—not get too far ahead of one another in maturity level. Randy tells me that they had a rip-roaring discussion recently about a "Dear Abby" column entitled "Growing Up Too Fast." A girl had written, "I'm in sixth grade. Many girls in my grade are into makeup, clothes, and boys. I have just recently gotten interested in those things too. But my friends haven't— they couldn't care less. What should I do?" Abby advises the writer to be patient; her friends will catch up.

But it isn't easy if you are either way ahead of or far behind your peers in middle school. One imagines that for these girls it is especially difficult if the popular kids have staked out the territory known as "cool and mature." The Goof Troop Girls feel incompetent, at least for now.

Do girls and boys want the same thing out of their group experience? Randy says there are differences. "The girls get the feeling of being in a group. The boys are just trying to fit in. They get to hear that they're not the only one. They're very problem-focused: 'How do I get Michael to leave me alone? How do I get him to stop flicking my ear?'" Indeed, the boys' sheets about what a friend does and doesn't do are all focused on social acceptance and the absence of teasing. For what a friend does, the boys wrote "Support you," "Be nice," "Have fun," "Go places with friends," and "Laughs at your jokes no matter how STOOPID they are." What a friend does not do: "Joke really personal," "Call you things that hurt your feelings," "Does not call you stupididiotjerk," and "Does not kick you in the shins." Boys are focused on avoiding getting "choked," as one put it.

If the Baha Boyz are just trying to survive, the girls are hoping to get back into the ring. Randy says, "The girls still want to be popular. They want friends. In sixth grade the girls are becoming aware of their bodies and their sexuality. They are very touchy, heads on each other's shoulders. They write long, intertwining notes to each other about who should sit with whom at lunch. The very popular girls link arms to show, 'She's my friend. I'm with her. She likes me.' " Linking arms in the casual way the popular girls do is not so easy for the Goof Troop Girls. "They are awkward," Randy says. They come to their group, in part, to learn how to be more socially at ease.

One girl who came to a meeting of the girls' group did not return because of her social ambition. When she realized that there was a rule of confidentiality, she said she couldn't abide by it. Her hope, apparently, had been that she could go to the meetings and be a source of information for the popular girls—and she said as much. "If I want to tell the popular girls what we say about them, I'm going to." She couldn't trade away her hope that she might be numbered among the most popular kids in the class. The sad thing, of course, was that she fell between the two groups and remained isolated, waiting by the phone for the call from the very popular kids that would never come.

Do the popular girls care what The Girls say about them in the lunch group? Absolutely not! Are the popular kids even aware of the Goof Troop Girls? Randy says they are aware but they don't allow themselves to be interested. "They don't really know about it, except they *do* know about it. High-status girls are in need of a group experience but can't touch it with a ten-foot pole."

Randy reminds us that, after all, even the girls at the top are simply sixth and seventh graders, filled with all the insecurities all children experience. In some ways their status cuts them off from getting help. The "cool" crowd is capable of becoming seriously isolated from the adult world because they read only their own press notices and think they're more hip than adults are. Though Randy can see their developmental struggles, the cool crowd at her school is something of a closed book to this veteran counselor. "My group of girls are the girls who struggle and who are very independent. They're the volleyball players, not the cheerleaders," she says. "I'm not sure what it is that makes the cheerleaders. They seem to feel better about themselves than my girls do."

The eternal mystery—for parents, counselors, and teachers—is why some children radiate social confidence and other children, good kids, don't have the ease, the self-esteem, the factor X that makes it possible for them to be as confident as the cheerleaders.

If a number of Randy's kids are socially inept, how does the group work? How can they teach one another skills that none of them possesses in abundance? Randy invited one pretty high-status kid to join the boys' group. His mother was wary and called to ask Randy about the invitation. Randy simply said, "He doesn't need to come." But the boy was intrigued by the idea. He came to the group and grew into his role as a regular and a teacher of the other boys. "He's a compassionate kid," Randy says, "and he gets something from the group. He also sets them right about some things they don't understand." This boy is a liaison—an ambassador—between the high-status boys and the low-status boys. He explains the motivations of the cool crowd and advises the Baha Boyz about how not to annoy the other boys.

How does the group handle a really difficult kid—a rejected-aggressive boy? Randy says, "I have one boy who is very provocative. You want a boy like this in the group, but he's hard to manage." When the boys participated in the "What are you looking for in a friend?" exercise, he wrote, "I want a friend who is very rich and can buy me a lot of things." That kind of in-your-face, defensive response is intended to denigrate the exercise and the feelings of the others. But the boys took him on. They tried to tell him why what he had written was ugly and defensive. "I don't think we ever got through to him, but at least he heard it from the kids. If I had said anything to him, it would have been an adult point and he wouldn't have heard it at all."

This boy sometimes comes to the lunch meetings with a book and makes a point of reading it while he eats, acting as if the conversation means nothing to him. He's not the only boy who has ever come to one of Randy's groups with a book behind which to hide. Many of these kids are socially uncomfortable to begin with. They may not read social cues as easily as other students in their class, and without a doubt, a majority of them have experienced some rejection by the more popular kids. It is not surprising that they engage in self-protective maneuvers. Because in Randy's groups participation is voluntary, there is an atmosphere of tolerance that makes it possible for children to be who they are when they are at the lunch group. One boy comes week after week and simply listens. He rarely speaks. But he has a job: He is the self-appointed timekeeper and announces when the lunch period is over. Now everyone has come to depend on him and would be startled if he did not remind them when it was time to stop talking and return to class.

We're left with three or four questions to ask our dedicated guidance counselor. What does the future hold for The Girls and the Baha Boyz? Will they be excluded forever? Do the teasing and marginalizing continue in high school?

Randy Pike thinks not. "When they turn fifteen or sixteen, when they can drive and get to places on their own, things get better," she says.

Does having a lunch group one day a week make a significant difference in a child's life? Randy replies, "Without the group, there would be three or four of these kids who would *always* eat alone, or one boy who would *always* sit with the girls, or one child who would *always* sit with the teachers. The group gives them one day a week when they have the interaction with other kids, one day a week when they feel accepted by a group." Yet when school districts cut their budgets, guidance counselors who have the imagination and will to put together groups like these are often the first ones fired.

During a brief meeting with a couple of the students from the Baha Boyz and The Girls the kids confirmed Randy's assessment of what the groups have done for them. Patrick said, "On the popularity scale the Baha Boyz are the people in the middle and on the bottom. But I have my friends; that's all I want." He admitted that before he joined, "I had pretty low self-confidence. Now I'm a lot more social."

Claire, who admitted to being shy, said that the group has helped her with conflict resolution: "I got in a fight with one of the girls in the group, but we went to work it out together." What was the net effect? "It has gotten me stronger and more confident."

Melissa may not have needed the group as much as others before she joined; she had been "a big part of a clique," she says. However, she had also been exclusive and would not have previously socialized with the kids from The Girls. The group sessions have helped her to separate from her previous crowd and have given her a new philosophy. "Now I feel more individual and not so dependent on everyone else. It helps you realize that the real world isn't always about you and your friends, and you have to get over that fact."

Randy is quite willing to reveal some of her personal motivation for leading these groups, for looking after isolated middle-school children all these years. Here's what she said: "Just be careful with what you write about the cheerleader stuff. I'm still scared of the cheerleaders. I'm a cheerleader wanna-be."

Harassed out of School

There is nothing about Ginny that suggests an easy target for harassment. She is an articulate, confident, blond, and beautiful seventeen-year-old girl who, when she uncurled from the couch and rose to say hello, stood a full six feet two inches tall. Perhaps the two boys who tormented her went after her precisely because she was so tall and Amazonian in their eyes. Perhaps they couldn't stand the combination of good looks, good fortune, and promising future that she radiates. That's what her mother thinks. "She's really beautiful, and she's very unattainable to these guys. The hate and envy really come out." Perhaps it was because the boys come from single-parent families who are struggling economically, living on the backside of a mountain covered with prosperous homes.

Ginny and her parents had agreed to meet with me to discuss the ordeal that drove her out of Jackson High School in mid-October, right before Halloween. She had been in her new school, St. Mary's, for a month and was liking it enormously. She was getting straight A's for the first time in her high school career, even though St. Mary's is considered a more academically challenging school than Jackson. All three of them attributed her improved grades to her new sense of safety. Though Ginny was beginning to feel okay, her parents were understandably still shocked and somewhat jumpy. When they sent her to their local high school, they had never imagined that they would have to call on the local police, have to go to the principal's office to withdraw her, and fight with their neighbors about whether or not she was responsible for getting two boys into trouble because she "told" on them. And they had lost some adult friends as a result of the uproar at school and the suspensions.

Had her problems started at the beginning of junior year? "Yeah," Ginny says, "except that it was like through freshman and sophomore year too. Freshman year wasn't that bad. It was just the nagging and the teasing. Sophomore year I had a lot of stickers of bands on my car, and the guys started coming up to me and telling me that I didn't like the right bands. I rode bikes and I had a bike rack on the back of my car, and they said I was trying to be an earth woman. . . . That wasn't that bad, I mean, because they'd come up to my window and they'd sit there and scream at me or I'd be driving out of the parking lot and they'd get in big groups and scream at me out of the parking lot, but that didn't, you know . . . it hurt, yeah, it hurt, but I kind of blew that off a lot."

Who were the boys she finally felt she had to report? Why did they attack her? It is a complex story, not easy to unravel, and, of course, it is told here from only one point of view: Ginny's. We have to speculate about the motivation of the boys. Ginny had gone to elementary school with them. She had been in class with them for years. In her mind they went after her because "I drove a car and everybody knew that my parents paid for my car . . . I had a problem this year when they gave us the list of fees on the first day of school and I had the money for the fees on the second day of school. It was a hundred and fifty dollars' worth of fees and I got them all in on the second day. And lunch tickets—whenever I got a lunch ticket, I'd always pay like fifty dollars so I wouldn't have to worry about getting checks from Mom. So they would notice that."

When asked if she thought she was significantly wealthier than the two boys, she acknowledged that she might be. "I don't know. I think Frank's family covers it up, but they live in a big house. I know Jerry; his parents are divorced and they just rent. I am a little bit more wealthy than them." Did she think there was economic stress in the boys' families? Ginny nodded. "Yes."

Does class warfare begin in high school? Of course it doesn't. By sixth or seventh grade children are aware of who has what, who wears new clothes, and who has a fancy house. Socioeconomic disparities do create tensions in a public school, but for the most part they remain under control. That is the central vision of public education: that all children, from all levels of life, can and should be educated together and made into citizens together. For the most part it worked for Ginny. Indeed, even if she liked the wrong bands and had a bike rack on the back of the car that her parents paid for, Ginny was still mostly okay during ninth and tenth grades.

So what was it that triggered the harassment that drove her out of the school? She tried to climb the social ladder into the most popular group.

Ginny received an invitation in the spring of her tenth-grade year that turned sour, and things went from bad to worse after that. "What set it all off was I went to Florida for spring break with four or five of the most popular girls in the school. That was kind of different for me. At first I was hesitant about going, because I was kind of wondering why I was going with that group, but then again I was excited because that was a new chance for me. So I went ahead."

She went to Panama City, Florida (now one of the great spring break destinations for high school groups from across the eastern United States) and stayed in a hotel that also housed a group of the most popular boys from her high school. During a party one of the boys, the president of his class at Jackson High, was quite drunk and stole her sunglasses, a $150 pair of Oakleys that had been a gift from her father. When she learned that he had them she tried to get them back, first appealing to the other girls for help, then to some boys, and then finally to their adult chaperone. The mother who had accompanied them to Panama City was no help. She had no control over the boys—or the girls, for that matter. She was, in the opinion of Ginny's father, a bit of an adolescent herself. Ginny reported, "I asked the lady that was in charge of us to help me out on this one and try to get the glasses back for me because I wasn't as superior as she was. She was kind of in charge of us, but that didn't happen and nobody was really on my side, so I had to call my dad. So from then on it was a big ordeal, and Dad had to call the guy's mother, and they had this talk. It was like the whole trip was me whining about my sunglasses. It was not fun, and from then on they thought I was a big tattletale."

Was Ginny excluded because of a pair of sunglasses? It seems too trivial a thing to account for what happened. Her father provided another explanation: "The social move up was because she had a car. They needed an extra car to get down there, and none of those girls could drive. I wasn't going to let her drive to Florida. But they didn't know that, so they invited her." And by the time they discovered that she wasn't going to be able to drive them, it would have been too rude to rescind the invitation. They couldn't say to her, "Look, we just invited you to exploit you for your car. Now that your parents won't let you drive, we've decided that you're not really popular enough to hang with us." But that was the truth.

Ginny's dad looked at her. He said he didn't want to summarize for her or contradict her, but he clearly wanted to explain that he came to understand, sooner or later, that the invitation from the popular group had not been genuine. "It was clear to me that she . . ." He hesitated. "She went down there without a car. And the popular kids dumped her."

Ginny jumped back into the narrative: "In the morning they'd go down to the beach without me. They'd just go out to eat without me. That is intentionally hurtful."

It turned out that Ginny hadn't joined in on all of the partying that the popular kids were doing. Her refusal to participate put their reputations at risk, because she was not similarly exposed. They needed to retaliate for that. Ginny continues, "There was a bunch of stuff that they did down there that was ridiculous but it was all, like . . . um . . . skinny-dipping in the ocean, all sorts of getting drunk—you know what I mean. Just like what people would do when they got drunk and what happened at the clubs down there, and just all sorts of stuff."

Ginny's boyfriend drove down to Florida to get her in the middle of spring break week. She didn't want to stay with the popular girls; she didn't want to drive back with them. But at the same time she felt guilty for leaving because her participation meant that the per-person cost for the hotel was lower. Her departure would cost all of them money. They had abandoned her, but she didn't want to abandon *them*.

When she returned to school after break, Ginny found that the popular girls had beaten her to the storytelling punch. At first she didn't know how to respond when people sidled up to her and provocatively asked, "So, Ginny, how was the trip?" Soon she learned that all of the stories about skinny-dipping featured her, and that in others she was the source of all the other girls' problems. "Everything they said, it kind of went back to me. You know, every story, I was there somehow, whether it was 'Yeah, we all went to the club, but Ginny wouldn't go' or 'Yeah, we all went out to eat but Ginny wouldn't sit by us,' or 'You know, because of Ginny we couldn't go somewhere.'" In the retelling of the trip she was a tattletale and a wet blanket. Still, things remained relatively calm until the end of the year.

In retrospect, Ginny knew she had made a terrible mistake to try to move into the exclusive social group at Jackson High. "I mean, the first time that I ever slept over at one of those girls' houses was the night before we left for that trip. It was just weird. I had never been with those girls, never had gone out with those girls to a party or anything."

She looked forward to coming back to school in the fall. "Yeah, I was really excited. I was going to be a junior, I was really comfortable with the school—you know, it's a big year. It started off pretty good, but then I parked next to one of the girls who went to Panama City with me, Kimberly. Kimberly asked me to walk her to her class, and we were talking and I thought that was great."

Ginny's longings to be part of the popular group were

emerging once again. Then one day in the parking lot two boys, Frank and Jerry, screamed at her. In front of a crowd of about twenty-five kids they jumped on her car, one of the boys on the hood, the other on the back, and taunted her. "They had like twenty-five people. I couldn't move, and I wasn't about to get out of the car. I think they were just trying to get me to say something back to them. I was nothing to them. Not once did Frank or Jerry ever come up to me alone. They were always in groups of two and three.

"The first time they jumped on the car I blew it off. The second time I was kind of like, 'Okay, this is getting out of hand.' I went to the administration. There were about twenty-five to fifty kids out in the parking lot around my car. They were all standing there looking at me, wondering— 'Something is going to happen, let's see what she does,' you know—and I'm freaking out. As I got in my car they broke out laughing, and when I put my car in reverse I heard glass breaking." The boys had put a beer bottle under her tire, and as she tried to drive away one of them kicked out her taillights.

That's when Ginny broke the adolescent code of silence in a very public way. She drove up to the front of the school and told the security guard what had happened to her car. The next morning when Jerry arrived at school, he was escorted to the principal's office and given a ten-day suspension. Then he apparently mouthed off to the vice principal and earned himself an extra five days of suspension. His friend Frank felt bad because it was he, in fact, who had kicked out the taillights. While they had both put the bottle under the wheel, it was Jerry who paid the price for both actions. Frank admitted to a guidance counselor that he felt bad about the injustice. The guidance counselor did not tell the administration; she made the decision to respect Frank's confidentiality.

Ginny's mother said, "The counselor left it up to Frank to notify the assistant principal, which he never did. That really would have gotten him suspended, and he never called up, never got into any trouble." Frank fell through the cracks of the disciplinary system and stayed in school to initiate, aggravate, and be the ringleader. He attempted to redress the injustice to his friend by rabble-rousing the kids to attack the tattletale girl, Ginny.

Ginny's father, an organizational consultant to businesses, stepped back in to explain the dynamics in the last phase of his daughter's ordeal. As troubled as he was, Frank, working alone, might not have been successful in routing Ginny from the school. He was aided by Peter, the class president. This was the same boy who had drunkenly stolen Ginny's glasses the previous spring in Panama City and passed them to another boy, who passed them to yet another boy. As Ginny and her parents learned later, the class president and the popular girl, Kimberly, authorized an all-out war on Ginny. And Frank was their perfect enforcer. He had been suspended from school ten times already. He was in a court-appointed rage control course. The father learned that he had, only two weeks previously, beaten up his sister and keyed his mother's car. Frank was a very angry boy; now he had the full backing of the popular kids for whatever he wanted to do to Ginny.

It was Frank's girlfriend, Karen, who attacked next. When Ginny arrived in her car the following day, Kimberly and Karen were sitting in Kimberly's car. As Ginny began to get out of her car, Karen started systematically slamming Kimberly's car door into Ginny's car, over and over with great force. Kimberly's car was larger, and the weight of its door inflicted considerable damage on the side of Ginny's car. Ginny sat there for a couple of minutes in disbelief, not knowing what to do. Once Karen had stopped, Ginny went and told the assistant football coach, who went looking for the two girls. They were nowhere to be found; they had skipped out of school after the incident. The next morning the assistant principal came to get Kimberly out of her first class. (Karen, being wiser in these matters, had not come to school at all.) As he escorted her out of class Kimberly began sobbing and continued crying all the way down the hall to the office. She was suspended for skipping school the previous day—and her dramatic weeping was the talk of the school.

After that the abuse of Ginny became a flood. One girl told her, with great vehemence, "Ginny, you should die!" That afternoon Frank sought her out as she stood with two friends. He screamed at her, "Ginny, you're such a bitch." He went on and on, blaming her for getting Jerry and Kimberly in trouble with the school authorities. Ginny looked to her two friends for help and realized that it was not going to be forthcoming; the girls were backing away from her both physically and psychologically. Finally the class valedictorian came up to her with a warning: "Ginny, you have to watch your back. They are planning to get you."

That was on a Friday afternoon. Ginny's parents decided over the weekend that they couldn't send her back to school. They called the principal and made an appointment for eight o'clock the following Monday.

Ginny's father said, "I was really upset. The girl who used

the word *die* had really stepped it up to the next level. The principal wanted the names of the two girls who had threatened Ginny. He asked me many times. Ginny had begged us not to do anything that would get the girls expelled. We didn't give him the names."

Ginny's father came away with the impression that the principal was helpless to fix the situation; indeed, he seemed to be asking the father's advice about how to handle it. Some time into the hour-and-a-half-long meeting, her parents asked for Ginny's transcripts to be sent over to St. Mary's, along with a letter of explanation.

Ginny started at St. Mary's the next day, and her family began to recover from their collective distress and trauma. But it is not entirely over. Ginny's father said, "I got a phone call eleven days later, from a pot-smoking kid's mother, saying that Ginny is causing him problems. She calls me up! I'm still reeling, trying to get our life together. And this is a member of our church whose son smokes pot regularly and got caught with Ecstasy very close to the school. She calls me up very angrily, eleven days after Ginny started at St. Mary's and our life finally is getting better. I'm taking a hot bath, and she tells me that my daughter is getting her son in trouble and will she please stop it and that Ginny was not innocent in all this. She just really went off on me. Now Ginny's the universal scapegoat for Jackson High School. She is everybody's number one suspect. I think my first thought is, 'Where are the parents of any of those kids?' "

What is the moral of this story? Is it that it is a challenge for educators to run a huge high school that contains all kinds of children from all kinds of homes? Is it that the popular crowd, the class president, can encourage the scapegoating of a child? That a crowd of good kids can turn into a mob? Is it that adults have very few tools for dealing with the social lives of adolescents? Is it, as Ginny's father believes, that the atmosphere of a school makes harassment possible?

We would be dismayed if the reader simply concluded from this story that Catholic schools are better than public schools. There is shocking social cruelty in church-run schools, and there are wonderful public schools where children feel safe. Ginny's story points up that events can spin out of control in the social lives of children when no one feels responsible or in control. Once a child has become a target, it is very difficult for other children to empathize with his or her situation. Even after Ginny was gone, her former classmates still didn't get it. A number of them came up to her on the street or in the neighborhood and said, in genuine astonishment, "We never thought you would ever leave the high school."

Because Ginny's parents had resources and were paying attention, they were able to get her into a new situation. But what would she have done if her parents had not been able to do that for her? She might have turned truant; she might have dropped out. She might have become a social recluse, or worse. It is the responsibility of adults in schools to make sure that students like Ginny—indeed, all students—are safe. It is not easy, but it must be done.

QUESTIONS & ANSWERS

Be a Parent, Not a Kid

Q: *One of the other seventh-grade moms at my son's school came storming onto the playground at recess one day, crying and yelling at some boys she accused of teasing her son and leaving him out of a weekend Rollerblading party. (I'm a library volunteer and heard the whole thing.) She also walked up to some parents in the parking lot that afternoon and chewed them out. I think her son was terribly embarrassed. My own son made me promise I would never do something like that! What do you think about parents taking on their kids' battles that way?*

A: Stories like that make me cringe for the adult *and* for the child involved. Some parents find it very tempting to get emotionally and actively involved in the battle zones of friendship, popularity, and social cruelty on behalf of their child. I call this "going back to middle school," and it is a bad idea. I cannot stress strongly enough that it doesn't pay, for you or your child, to go back to middle school—or to high school or elementary school, for that matter.

The most extreme case of going back to school that I have come across recently was written up in the *Boston Globe* last year. A high school junior was allegedly slapped by a former student during school hours. The odd thing about this fight was that the assailant stormed into the school with her mother, who apparently encouraged and supported the attack.

Most of the situations I deal with of parents going back to middle school or high school are not quite so extreme. For instance, a parent goes overboard to ensure that her child throws the best parties, wears the best clothes, gives the best gifts, has the best toys. This is not a matter of keeping up with the group by buying the shoes that everyone has in order not to be left out. This is pulling out all the stops to give a child an advantage in the popularity wars.

Other examples abound: A parent gossips about other children and their parents with her child, or with other parents. A mom is so eager to be considered cool by her daughter's popular friends that she serves them alcohol. A dad wants to be one of the gang, so he takes the boys to a porno movie or smokes marijuana with them. Even more commonly, parents may turn a blind eye to kids getting drunk or high in their house because they don't want to risk being uncool. Be a parent, not a kid.

The social milieu of the school can spill over into adults' lives as well. A school that has a problem with cliques among the students often has cliques among the parents as well. Queen bee daughters often have queen bee moms, who may exclude other parents from their in-group. When parents develop a circle of friends because their kids are in school together, that's great. But not speaking to certain parents or snubbing them in the parking lot is not great.

Then there are the parents who host birthday parties or sleepovers that leave some children out—for example, allowing children to invite every girl in the class except one, or to invite every white child and none of the children who are not white. In one school a parent complained about her daughter not being invited to a special party that included everyone else on the soccer team. The parents giving the party relented and the excluded girl came, only to discover when her mother picked her up that everyone else but her had been invited to sleep over.

A mother sent us this e-mail about going back to elementary school: "My daughter was looking forward to Brownies [the first level of Girl Scouts] all summer before second grade, and she made me fill out the application form the day it came in the mail. Shortly before the first meeting, we received a list of who was in the troop, which was based at the school. I noticed that every girl in her class was on the list, except for three recent immigrants to the United States. I called the mom who was the Scout leader and left a message saying that I thought this was probably due to a language and cultural barrier—these new immigrant families probably didn't understand the letter or appreciate that all the other girls would be involved. I then made an effort to talk to the moms of the three excluded children after school. Once I explained about Brownies they were all interested. But the troop leader called back and said it was too late—they had missed the deadline. I was appalled. I asked if there could be a meeting of the parents to discuss this. (I was trying to be calm and not give a furious lecture on diversity and respect.) She agreed to the meeting, but when I showed up, it was clear that she had called several powerful moms in the class and was prepared to steamroll any opposition so that the nonwhite, foreign-born girls would not be allowed into Brownies. These moms all pretended that the deadline for applying to the troop was a sacred oath and that racism had nothing to do with it. When I pointed out that Brownies was meeting on school property and therefore shouldn't even appear to discriminate, they said they'd meet at the troop leader's house instead!"

The most common way that fathers get into the action of going back to school is by pressuring their sons to participate or excel in sports, because they are trying to live out their own unfulfilled dreams. I read recently that a majority of Little League fathers think their sons "have what it takes" to go professional, even though less than 1 percent will even play ball in college.

I hope that these examples serve as cautionary tales to help you think twice about reliving your own childhood and adolescent social experiences through your children. However, it is possible to be involved in constructive ways in a child's social world without going back to middle school (or elementary or high school). Finding out from teachers or the principal how your child is doing socially, for example, and asking how you can help if things are not going well, are perfectly appropriate parental responses. In the same way, it makes sense to check in with other parents about what they are allowing or not allowing in terms of independence (to find out when other kids are allowed to go alone to the pizza parlor, or trick-or-treat without parents, or watch R-rated movies). Most children will tell their parents, "Everyone else gets to do it," so it's wise parenting to do a reality check. Finally—and this probably goes without saying—being actively involved in your child's school, on the PTO or as a volunteer, is not the same as "going back to middle school."

A Boy Marches to the Beat of a Different Drummer

Q: *My son has always been an outsider at school. He says he doesn't want to be part of the in-group, but I think he's pretty lonely and I know he gets teased a lot. It has gotten so bad that we are thinking of taking him out of the public school in our neighborhood and looking for a school that would be a better fit for him and where he could get a fresh start socially in sixth grade. Do you have any ideas on what to look for in a school for him? He's a great kid, but he has always marched to the beat of a different drummer. At the school where he is now it seems that everyone marches to exactly the same beat except him.*

A: Your concern touches on a question both parents and school administrators ask often: When, if ever, should you change schools to help a child's social situation? In looking for a school for an individualist like your son, do you go with a school that values individuality, where he has a better chance of being accepted? Or do you go with a school that stresses group identity, where he has a better chance of being encouraged to participate in group life?

For most families, the decision to change schools for social reasons does not come easily. The idea of a fresh start has to be weighed against the drawbacks of being the new kid on the block. Classmates can have long memories (like the kids who still tease a ninth grader about wetting his pants in first grade). But they can be hard on newcomers, too.

I think I have seen about every possible outcome of this situation, so I don't have any simple answers. I have seen children stay in their school and thrive as their peers grow up, mature, and become more tolerant of differences. I have seen children stay in their school and remain miserable, stuck in roles as scapegoats or outcasts. I have seen children move to a new school and flourish, and I have seen them move to a new school and be treated even worse than before.

Because this decision is so complex and the outcomes so variable, my main advice is to get help in making the decision from someone outside the family who knows your child well. Children and parents are often too close to the situation, and a guidance counselor, family friend, therapist, or educational consultant can provide much-needed perspective.

One reason an outside perspective is so important is that you and your child might think there's nothing to lose, that things could never get worse and are not likely to get better. But an outsider might have a clearer picture of the child, the current school, and other schools. Besides, he or she is not caught up in the immediate painfulness of the situation. Sometimes a child may be depressed because of his social situation (or other reasons) and as a result of the depression just shrugs and says he doesn't care if he goes to school or what happens to him. Or a child might insist that everything is fine when it really isn't. Again, people at school or in your extended family who know your child well can provide perspective.

You say your son marches to the beat of a different drummer. That being the case, the most important feature to consider in a new school is the way it balances the needs of the individual with the needs of the group. Obviously, children who are different from the crowd need a school where differences are tolerated, even valued. Many great thinkers have said that you can judge a society by how it treats its lowest-status members: the poor, the imprisoned, the mentally ill. The same can be said of a school. How safe do children feel who look different, dress different, act different? Some schools are tolerant and accepting in certain areas, such as economic or religious differences, but intolerant in other areas, such as homosexuality.

Even in schools with strong traditions and values promoting individuality, middle school can be a time of strong pressure for everyone to be like everyone else. My friend's son, Anthony, goes to a very progressive school that prides itself on its encouragement of individuality and self-expression. Anthony has a unique style in his clothes, his attitudes, and his taste in books and music. In the third, fourth, and fifth grades he was a valued and respected member of his class. He didn't gain any converts to his styles or preferences, but he was acknowledged as unique rather than being rejected as different. But on the first day of sixth grade, when Anthony showed up at school with new blond streaks in his hair, a friend and classmate turned around and walked away without a word when Anthony said hello. At first Anthony thought the other boy just hadn't heard him, so he said hello louder. Still no answer. Finally he walked right up to him and asked what was up. The boy turned around, looked Anthony up and down, and said, "Your hair is stupid, those necklaces you wear are stupid, and your clothes are stupid," and walked away.

Welcome to sixth grade. The imperatives of group cohesion can temporarily override the school's values of tolerance and diversity.

Some schools make thoughtful efforts to offset the conformity of middle school. For example, at Wayland Middle School in Wayland, Massachusetts, the sixth grade spends the year studying Henry David Thoreau, the rugged individualist, as an antidote to the onslaught of middle-school groupthink. They follow that up in seventh grade by focusing on Rachel Carson, the environmentalist, to combat middle-schoolers' tendency to be absorbed in their own little worlds. In eighth grade Dr. Martin Luther King Jr. is held up as the class mentor, as a way of going against the tide of tribalism that separates subgroups from one another.

I admire your wish to find a school where your son can thrive. Talk to as many people as you can as you search. Talk to parents, to kids, to counselors, to graduates of the school. And make sure to include your son in the conversation.

The Tattletale

Q: *Why do children tattle on each other, and what can I do to get them to stop?*

A: I think we adults often give children mixed messages about tattling. We want them to tell us certain things, and we get very bent out of shape when a group of children knows about a serious problem and no one steps forward. But at the same time we belittle those children who come to us as "tattletales." There are things we want to know about and things we would just as soon not have to deal with, and we can't expect children to automatically know the difference.

We tell younger children to go to a teacher instead of throwing a punch, but when they do, we tell them not to be a tattletale. We tell older children to work things out for themselves, but then we are horrified that children keep their classmates' secrets about life-threatening things such as guns, drugs, or anorexia. I think the answer to this confusion is to make a clear distinction between telling an adult in order to protect someone's safety or to get needed help versus telling an adult to get someone in trouble. The former is a basic safety strategy; the latter is tattling. Of course, it isn't always so easy to sort out those two motives.

With that said, there are actually many reasons why a particular child might be prone to telling tales. A child who tattles repeatedly may be asking for help in managing his or her status in the group. The child may be being excluded or marginalized and—not knowing how to make his or her way back in—tries to get adult help. Or the child may have felt betrayed by a friend and now it's payback time.

Children also tell on each other because they are working hard on figuring out how to control their own impulses. When they see another child act out an impulse instead of controlling it, they are outraged. When they run to the teacher to tattle, they are really seeking help with the emotional confusion and anxiety caused by watching another child do something they would very much like to do themselves. I think this explains why so-called Goody Two-shoes, who are totally inhibited about doing anything wrong, are often tattletales. They have those very same impulses that the "bad" kids have. It is intolerable for them to see a child act out one of those impulses—whether it's aggressive, disruptive, attention-seeking, or sexual—when they have their own impulses so tightly controlled. They can't let another child get away with something that their own conscience won't allow them to do.

Tattling is also a way to align oneself with the grown-ups. Children who are rejected or marginalized by the group often try to side with grown-ups, both out of revenge against the cruel kids who rejected them and because they need to belong with someone. But teachers and parents often feel quite ambivalent about this kind of behavior. On one hand it's seen as responsible and mature, but on the other hand it's seen as ingratiating and clinging. We want children to bond with other children, except when we want them to be "above" the level of the other children. No wonder kids are confused!

Another way to look at tattlers is to ask yourself if they're seeking your input or help because they have already tried to work things out and have reached an impasse, or whether it's an effort to short-circuit the important process of working things out for themselves. If they have tried on their own, you probably will want to offer some assistance. But make sure your assistance isn't just punishing the child who was tattled on. Instead, say something like, "Looks like you guys need some help figuring things out, since a lot of feelings are getting hurt." You can offer to go together and talk to the other child about what has been happening, with an emphasis on helping the tattling child assert himself or herself directly, rather than your speaking for them. That helps the child handle things on his or her own in the long run. On the other hand, if the child was trying to skip the process of working it out, you can't just tell the child not to be a tattle-tale and send him or her back to resolve the conflict or problem alone. The whole reason the child came to you is that he or she doesn't feel confident settling conflicts without adult help. The child may just need encouragement—or may need practice such as role-playing what he or she could say to the other child.

The Only Black Girl in Kindergarten

Q: *A couple of years ago I taught a kindergarten class that had only one black girl. Her name was Nicole. Some children didn't like to touch her, to hold hands or hug. It broke my heart to see Nicole face discrimination at her age. I wish I had specific information on how to deal with this situation—not only on one day, but also throughout the year. I would like to be able to change the children's perspectives and views in a permanent way.*

A: You were right to be upset. You were witnessing the beginnings of racial discrimination in your children. However, as a kindergarten teacher, you are in a position to affect the development of prejudice in your students. You can protect children like Nicole, and you can make a lifelong difference in the attitudes of your students. I applaud you for wanting to do so.

In her book *I'm Chocolate, You're Vanilla: Raising Healthy Black and Biracial Children in a Race-Conscious World*, Marguerite Wright talks about the way young children focus very concretely on skin color and only later think about race in more complex ways. They may think that skin color can rub off onto them or that a person's skin color can change. The terms *black* and *white* confuse them, since most people are neither of those colors. Being confused, and not being able to ask questions about it, makes them scared of the child who is different. It isn't racism, it's concrete thinking—but it can turn into racism if not guided properly. That means that teachers in younger grades have to talk specifically about these misconceptions and confusions.

There is an old song from the musical *South Pacific* called "You Have to Be Carefully Taught." It is sung by a Polynesian woman, and it is about prejudice. Here's how it goes: "You've got to be taught to hate and fear. You've got to be carefully taught." Research bears out the words of the song. Bigotry is taught. And once it is thoroughly inculcated, it is very hard to reverse the training. But a kindergarten teacher is there early enough in the lives of children to teach something different that may succeed in derailing the teaching of racial prejudice.

Children naturally react to differences in appearance. They notice anything that is a change from what they are accustomed to seeing. But this natural reaction to difference is not yet prejudice in its more adult form. Left on their own, children usually get past the differences between one another and start to play. For most kids, having someone with whom to play is far more important than anything as superficial as skin color.

Children are not naturally predisposed to be bigoted. Prejudice starts because children watch their parents carefully and absorb all the lessons that their parents teach, deliberately and unconsciously. Children see how their parents react to people with dark skin; they listen to what their parents and neighbors say about people of different nationalities or religions. They take their cue from the fears and hatreds of adults.

From the first day in your class, I would use activities that involve singing, dancing, and holding hands. Simply standing in a circle in the morning holding hands as a way of greeting the day would be a start. Every child in your class should easily hold the hand of any other child. A square dance that involves moving from hand to hand would make that happen right away. Once your students see other children holding the hand of a black girl, they will be less reluctant to do it themselves.

I doubt that a child will recoil from holding the hand of a black girl when all the other children are holding hands. If that should happen, I would say to that child, in front of all the other children, "It is important that we all be able to hold one another's hands in this class. We're all part of the same community, and we all have to learn to work together."

There also must be dolls of every color in your play corner. There must be posters and pictures on the walls that portray children of every race. And tolerance—no, more than tolerance, a celebration of difference—must be at the center of your curriculum. It's not enough just to tell kids not to be mean or exclusive. You have to make an extra effort to include everyone.

When you hold up a book that has a black girl as its heroine, you can ask the same kind of question you would about any child portrayed in any book: "What do we notice about her?" You would ask that if the book were about an Inuit child, a Japanese child, a child who lived on a farm, or a child from a nomadic culture. Frank acknowledgment of difference—and your comfort with all of the ethnic and racial variations in the world—will make an enormous difference in the attitudes of your children. Perhaps a child will say about the character in the book, "She looks like Nicole," referring to the black girl in your class. That might lead to a discussion about different skin colors. You then might be able to ask Nicole, "How does it feel to be the only black girl in the class? Do you feel that other children treat you differently?" You may be astonished by what she says. There is a very good chance that you will create many "teachable moments" like this one if you are matter-of-fact and comfortable with the subject of race.

Not every teacher is comfortable with leading such a discussion. If that is the case, you should prepare yourself to discuss race with children by talking to a colleague who is at ease with the subject, by reading a book, or by attending a workshop on race. Why do I believe that it is essential that teachers prepare themselves in this way? Because *not* to prepare is to collude silently in the racism of parents and children. No child can ever feel safe in the classroom of such a teacher.*

*Libraries and bookstores and Web sites are loaded with excellent resources on this topic. A few we would like to recommend are *White Teacher* and *Kwaanza and Me*, both by Vivian Paley, and the magazine *Teaching Tolerance*.

Not-So-Innocent Bystanders

Q: *We had an incident at our school recently where a couple of bullies beat up another boy very badly. I think the school has done a good job of dealing with the perpetrators and helping the victim, but it turns out that a large number of students knew it was going to happen and didn't report it to anyone. Afterward, even though they knew the boy was seriously injured, they still didn't say anything. These are good kids, but by their silence they did something really terrible. We're not sure how to handle it. Do you have any suggestions?*

A: You certainly hit the nail on the head by noting that these were good children who did something morally terrible—even though they weren't the ones to do the physical beating. A number of books have examined the effect on spirituality when bad things happen to good people. But what about when good people do bad things? That's much more complicated.

Social psychologists have identified a number of factors that help explain why bystanders, the silent majority, stay silent, and why more often than not they don't step in to help.

- **Diffusion of responsibility.** The study of the failure of innocent bystanders to help a victim of violence began with the horrible murder in New York of a woman named Kitty Genovese. Dozens of people heard her cries, but no one called the police or left their homes to try to help her. The researchers who interviewed the silent neighbors concluded that each person thought that helping was someone else's responsibility. In a school, each student might feel that someone else will tell, so they don't have to get involved.

- **Tribal differences.** In spite of all of our religious and moral teachings about loving our neighbor as ourselves and seeing the humanity in every one of our brothers and sisters, human beings still act tribally much of the time. Anyone who is different from us is a potential threat, and it is okay for them to be targeted. In a school setting, that might mean that a person labeled as a wimp, fag, geek, tattletale, Goth, cheerleader, or athlete is a legitimate target. If someone in my group attacks someone from another group, I may deplore the attack, but I will still be loyal to my group. Adults belong to a different tribe altogether, which explains why the students in your school did not reveal the plot or the aftermath of the beating to teachers or parents.

- **Group process.** The children who actually commit the violence or the worst of the social humiliation have a knack for getting everyone else to feel like an active or passive accomplice. That ensures that they don't tell or try to intervene. In addition, the ringleaders get the group to participate in, or approve of, lower-level attacks. Then they can't turn someone in without incriminating themselves.

- **Social distance.** This factor is similar to tribal differences. A person who is socially different from oneself, whether higher or lower on the ladder, is not considered to be a real part of one's life. Whatever happens to that person doesn't really matter.

- **Emotional distance.** Children—and adults—distance themselves emotionally from things they don't want to face. The students in your school who saw the beaten boy and then went about their business as usual were probably telling themselves, "This isn't real, it didn't happen, it's not that bad." The reality was so overwhelming that it didn't really sink in.

- **Authority approval.** When a school knows that cruelty and violence is occurring and nothing is done, or a perpetrator is slapped on the wrist, then the students take this as approval for the behavior and abandonment of the victims. Sadly, this is done most often with top athletes or winning sports teams. The pressure to let them keep competing is great, no matter what they might have done. At worst, these students feel they are above the rules and that they have the blessing of the community no matter what they do.

- **Myth of no consequences.** When social cruelty remains abstract and distant, it is easy to maintain the myth that there are no real consequences. That's why it is so important for schools to make it safe enough for victims to speak out, and to convey to perpetrators and bystanders that real people experience real suffering when cruelty goes on unchecked.

- **Bullies do the dirty work of the group.** Kids who are violent at school or in a neighborhood usually do not pick their victims at random. Instead they choose someone to beat on who won't be protected by the group or who has actually been "turned over" to the bully by the group. Victims are often people who are rejected, outcast, and picked on verbally or emotionally by the larger group. Most of the group members would never be violent themselves, but they give the most aggressive bullies the green light to target a few marginal students. The group as a whole may be unaware that they are silently condoning and even encouraging the violence of the most aggressive of the students.

I hope this list helps explain the moral failure of bystanders to protect their more vulnerable peers, and conveys the importance of schoolwide and communitywide programs for addressing social cruelty. Effective programs don't stop at identifying perpetrators and comforting victims. They have to take into account the largest group, the good kids in the middle who are capable of doing bad things under the right conditions.

Win-Win Leadership

Q: *I am a guidance counselor in a public school that goes from kindergarten to eighth grade. A few years ago there was an eighth grade boy who was by far the most popular kid in the grade, and indeed in the whole school. The amazing thing was that he was kind and friendly to everyone. He didn't abuse* *his power; he didn't start a clique; he didn't put people down. He genuinely liked people and they genuinely liked him. Almost every other alpha male and alpha female I have seen at the school has been mean, bossy, and/or power-hungry. I often wish I could bottle whatever it was that boy had and pass it out to a few select kids each year. Is there any way to get other students to be more like him?*

A: What a wonderful story—and I would love a percentage of the profits if you ever manage to patent and bottle that formula! That boy had good leadership skills, and you are absolutely right that the world is short on those. Without good leadership skills, leaders tend to rely on brute strength, intimidation, or manipulation.

To look even deeper, schools often don't really elect leaders at all. Instead, they rely on primitive struggles for popularity or dominance. Most often, popular kids are "elected" into a leadership position because of their looks, their athletic ability, their money, or some other characteristic that has nothing much to do with actual leading. And yet these popular students automatically assume leadership roles—both formal and informal—in every school. It's no wonder that the power often goes to their heads and they become destructive rather than constructive forces in the community.

I don't want to suggest that the boy you describe—the good leader—is absolutely unique. Good leaders can be found in every school, on lots of sports teams, and in many neighborhoods full of kids. But I am not surprised that you seldom see excellent leadership among eighth graders. Popularity and leadership are very different, and middle school is typically the peak of popularity's sway. Some people might argue that leadership is even less common and popularity even more of a force in adult politics than it is in middle school. But sixth, seventh, and eighth graders represent a special pinnacle of primitive Darwinism, in which looks, athletic ability, and financial resources determine a child's status.

Things change in high school. As one senior told me, "We still have our popular kids, but they aren't our leaders anymore." In other words, high school often signals a shift from leadership based on the primitive Darwinism of middle school to leadership based on more substantive criteria. The popular kids might retain their roles in terms of which clothes, styles, and music are cool, but the real leaders run the show. And the good ones have specific leadership skills and styles.

What are these leadership skills? You didn't say much about exactly how this boy managed his outstanding achievement of being an alpha male without being power-hungry or cruel. My guess is that he was an expert at what are called "win-win strategies." Those strategies can, and should, be taught—especially to student leaders and potential student leaders.

Win-win strategies have been described in a variety of areas, from business negotiating (*Getting to Yes* by Roger Fisher) to marriage counseling (*Getting the Love You Want* by Harville Hendrix). These same strategies apply to young people learning how to be effective leaders. The essence of a win-win interaction is that each person walks away happy, or at least content that their own opinions and feelings have been valued and adequately addressed. The opposite of win-win is often described as a "zero-sum game," in which someone must lose for someone else to win. That is, your loss plus my gain (or the other way around) adds up to zero. On the contrary, in win-win, everyone comes out ahead.

Some children are naturals at win-win. Jane says, "Let's play hide-and-seek," and Sue says, "Let's play with our dolls." Our win-win leader says, "Let's pretend that our dolls are playing hide-and-seek. Everybody get a doll and take it to hide." Across town, Joe says, "Hey Bill, you've been playing with that truck for a long time. It's my turn." Bill doesn't say, "Tough luck," which would inevitably lead to Joe grabbing the truck away or else threatening not to be Bill's friend anymore. Instead, Bill employs a win-win approach, "You're right! I'm sorry. Can I just finish this big crash, then you can have a long turn?" As you see, being a win-win expert requires flexibility, creativity, and a willingness to compromise. But it isn't as simple as "take turns," as many teachers and parents like to say. Real win-win strategies leave each person feeling good, while an injunction to share, or take turns, or be nice, often leaves both children feeling resentful.

Even children who aren't naturals at win-win can learn the concept. The important thing to remember when teaching it is to use lots of examples. Ask children to go over a conflict and say how they might have used win-win to have it come out differently.

A second aspect of effective leadership is listening. Good leaders are good listeners. They might have really good ideas, but if their ideas aren't immediately followed, they are able to listen to everyone else's ideas and make a proposal that takes everybody's thoughts and feelings into account. Good listeners reflect back what they have heard so that other people feel valued and respected.

Perhaps the most important quality of good leadership is empathy. Empathy is the ability to put oneself in someone else's shoes, to see things from the other person's perspective, to feel other people's pain and not just focus selfishly on one's own needs and desires. Some people are more empathic than others are, but everyone can be taught to be more empathic than they are already. Again, this teaching is best done through examples and discussions as opposed to moralistic lectures.

I have suggested teaching student leaders and potential leaders the skills they need to lead with kindness, compassion, effectiveness, and win-win outcomes. But you will notice that I haven't suggested that we encourage children and teenagers to choose leaders who already have these characteristics. It would be great if popularity were based on good leadership skills instead of on those surface characteristics of looks and dominance and money. But children and teenagers use their own criteria for choosing their leaders and their most popular peers, and leadership skills are not typically at the top of the list. It's a better bet to identify the leaders chosen by their peers and teach them good leadership. Even better, teach everyone, since all students—no matter what their status in the dominance hierarchy—can benefit from learning win-win strategies, empathy, and listening.

Every interaction between students or between kids in a neighborhood potentially can be a teaching moment for good leadership skills. In addition, your school might want to implement a specific leadership training curriculum, either for all students or for a select group who show leadership potential. Some schools have implemented peer counseling or peer mediation, which require teaching students these exact skills of listening, empathy, and win-win strategies.

This shift—from alpha males selected for their good looks or their brute strength to real leadership based on deeper qualities—always makes me think of a scene from the comedy sketch by Mel Brooks and Carl Reiner about the two-thousand-year-old man. Brooks "explains" the origins of religion back in the Stone Age. He says that they didn't have God, they had Phil. Phil was the biggest, meanest, toughest guy around. Everybody worshiped him. Reiner asks what happened. Brooks answers that one day Phil got struck by lightning. That led to the next stage of human spiritual development. Everyone said, "Hey, there's something bigger than Phil."

To Box or Not to Box

Q: *My husband wants to teach our son to box so he can fight back against the bullies who have been bothering him. I think that will just teach him to use his fists to solve problems. It goes against everything I believe in and everything I want for my son. Can you settle our argument?*

A: You're both right!

Whenever I talk with adults about childhood teasing and bullying, there is always at least one man who tells a story about deciding to fight back physically against bullying, usually after a long time of passively taking it. Often, even if he lost the fight, the bullying stops, because he wasn't seen as an easy mark anymore.

Some kinds of bullies get their satisfaction from seeing a victim cower and cry, so refusing to cave in can break that cycle. Your husband may be right that teaching your son to defend himself and feel strong will end his painful role as victim.

However, you are right that there is a fine line between encouraging children to stand up for themselves and justifying the use of fists to solve problems. Watching generation after generation of boys toughen up and lose their warm and tender side has made me wonder if there can't be another way to give boys a sense of security without making them fight for it. We have to give boys a wider range of choices than being either an ogre or a sissy. It helps to have a response that is systemwide, not just geared toward one child. For example, many schools teach nonviolent conflict resolution and expect children to practice what they learn.

For some children, good martial arts instruction helps them find this balance between sensitivity and strength. They learn how to defend themselves and develop confidence, but they also learn deeper philosophical principles about the uses and abuses of power. On a more basic level, some kids develop confidence just from being in a fistfight and seeing the worst that can happen. But it's tricky. Some boys may feel betrayed when their parents encourage them to fight back. They may well get clobbered—and then retreat further into misery and isolation. Moreover, some bullies don't stop just because the victim starts to fight back. Instead, they escalate the violence. So you must be very sure about what you're doing and whom you're dealing with.

Another potential problem, which I have seen all too often, is that when dads teach their sons to "defend themselves," the instruction may be based on humiliation and fear. The adult is out to toughen the boy up and is brutal about it. The teacher, whether a father, a big brother, a coach, or an instructor, is acting out his own insecurities about his own masculinity by taunting the boy about being slow or weak or a sissy. Of course, that makes things even worse for the boy.

An eighth-grade boy who had been in a lot of trouble at school for fighting told me that he "wasn't scared of anybody" because his two older brothers had taught him to box. It turns out that they had "taught" him by beating him up repeatedly and viciously. The boy bragged to me that he "didn't even feel pain anymore." He told me about getting a deep cut from a broken mirror he had punched in frustration and not feeling any pain. That is definitely not the kind of toughness we want to encourage when we think about helping boys protect themselves from bullies!

When I ran therapy groups for men who were in trouble with the law for violence against women or children I heard dozens of stories from them about being pressured into fighting when they were young boys by their fathers or their older brothers. One sad story was about a boy who ran home, chased by three large bullies. He ran into the house, thinking he was finally safe, and his mother sent him back outside and locked the door so he could "take his beating like a man." The saddest thing was that he told this story as though it was a badge of honor, that it had "made me into the man I am today." He did not see that the man he was today was violent, intimidating, and cruel.

Of course, that is an extreme case and not at all what your husband has in mind when he talks about teaching your son to box. The important distinction is this: What is the basic message behind the encouragement to fight? Is it for your son to be able to stand up for himself and protect others who are being mistreated? Or is it to be the toughest guy on the block, to punish anyone who dares disrespect him, to promote the idea that might makes right, and to glorify violence for its own sake? Fighting back can be a way to promote a healthy sense of oneself as safe and secure, as someone who deserves to be treated decently and fairly. Or it can promote the kind of false self-esteem that bullies have—a view of oneself as superior to others, as someone who must be feared and obeyed. If you focus on safety and self-confidence, then you don't have to worry that your husband's boxing lessons will turn your son into a violent monster.

Your values as a family are also crucial to this discussion. I can't tell you or your son whether it is better to turn the other cheek or better to stand up for yourself. That's a matter of your moral and spiritual values. It can be confusing if you would like your son to emphasize forgiveness and acceptance while your husband would like him to emphasize self-respect. So have some family discussions about courage. Does courage come from walking away from a fight or from standing your ground? What is strength? Is it being able to take what others dish out without stooping to their level or is it showing them that they can't push you around? What is confidence? Your son's thoughts about those questions can be a good guide to whether or not to teach him boxing and encouraging him to fight back.

Back in the 1970s and 1980s, assertiveness training courses were very popular, and for good reason, since most people tend to be either too passive or too aggressive. The funny thing about assertiveness is that it seems too strong to people who are inclined to be more gentle, and it seems too weak to people who are inclined to be more intense. In fact, assertiveness is just right. It's like the old chemistry class trick of putting one hand in ice water and one hand in hot water, then putting both hands into the same bucket of water at room temperature. The exact same water feels both hot and cold, depending on what you are used to.

For you, boxing lessons feel like your husband is shoving your son into a tough world of street fighting. For your husband, your approach feels like you are coddling your son and dooming him to be an eternal victim. In between are real assertiveness, real strength, and real confidence.

Before we leave this topic, I want to talk about the controversy at some schools about whether to encourage formal boxing matches as an alternative to fistfights and brawls. There is a long-standing tradition in British boarding schools, followed by some schools in the United States, to settle disputes among boys by putting them in a boxing ring with boxing gloves and referees and official rules. I have heard differing reports about the success of this approach. Some men say that it helped them control their aggression or earned them the respect of the group, while others say that it just made their humiliation more public and profound. The difference, I think, is in whether there is a big power imbalance between the two kids. Are the boxing gloves and official rules going to even up the match, or at least make it more even than it was? Or is it still a terrible mismatch that will be humiliating for one of the kids?

Last year in Brockton, Massachusetts, the hometown of prizefighters Rocky Marciano and Marvin Hagler, a high school principal organized an "official" fight between two boys who had been getting into lots of fistfights. He was afraid the boys were going to escalate their arguments into using knives or guns. He thought a fair fight, supervised by him, would be a better alternative. Not surprisingly, it was a highly controversial decision. He claimed afterward that it was successful, that the boys now know and respect each other in a new way. Many others in the community felt that the fight sent the wrong message to kids, as well as deliberately jeopardizing the safety of the two boys. Some said the only problem was that he didn't provide boxing gloves.

But that case was not about a bully and a victim. If a conflict is about two boys burning off aggression, it might make sense to have them put on boxing gloves and get into the ring and follow the rules of boxing, instead of beating each other up with bare fists in the parking lot. But if it's a matter of victimization, then the boxing ring approach just cements the humiliation of the weaker person.

Our goal is to help our children feel safe without having to be violent. For some kids, learning self-defense is an important part of that sense of safety and confidence.

When the Bullies Are Winning

Q: *My son has come home from school totally miserable almost every day this year. For months he just locked himself in his room and turned his music up real loud. I finally got him to tell me what was happening, and it turns out that he was being bullied by a group of three boys with one clear ringleader. I went straight to the school but all I got from the administration was a song and dance about how bullies have low self-esteem and they were taking care of it. But they are not taking care of it. It just keeps going on. It looks to me like the bullies are running the school, and it's my son who has the low self-esteem. How can I get through to the school?*

A: A couple of years ago my colleague Sam Roth and I met with a group of eighth graders in a public school outside Boston. The students had been selected by their principal to participate in a Teasing and Bullying Task Force. During one of the first meetings the students had an impassioned argument about whether bullies have low self-esteem and just need to be understood or whether they have too high an opinion of themselves and need to be taken down a peg or two.

I was impressed by this discussion because I had been busy reading the research literature on bullying, and it turns out the professionals in the field have been having the same argument. For many years, most psychologists and educators assumed that bullies have low self-esteem that leads them to act aggressively toward their peers. Then Dan Olweus, the preeminent researcher into bullying behavior, actually studied the issue. He found that most bullies have an inflated sense of their own self-worth. Of course, it may be that underneath that inflated self-esteem there is a deeper unconscious feeling of self-hatred or inadequacy, but that is hard to measure. On the level that can be measured, Olweus found bullies to have low levels of anxiety and insecurity. He also debunked the myth that bullies are just cowards who don't really want to fight and thus only intimidate little or weak kids. In fact, bullies are just as likely to pick a fight with someone the same size or even bigger than they are. We only call it bullying, however, when the power or strength is really one-sided. On the other hand, it is true that most bullies were once the victims of bullying themselves, from fathers, older brothers, or bigger boys. There has never been a bully baby!

But if bullies have high self-esteem, then self-esteem isn't all it's cracked up to be. In fact, I think that this controversy shows that self-esteem is not really a useful concept for understanding bullies and victims. There is a good kind of self-esteem, which involves respect for oneself and others, and a bad kind of self-esteem, which is selfish and domineering. That's the risk of being repeatedly victimized, isn't it? That a child not only will feel afraid and anxious but also come to believe he or she deserves to be mistreated. In fact, victims of bullies are more likely than other children to become depressed when they are young adults. But the vast majority recovers once the bullying stops and they develop good-quality friendships. The outlook isn't nearly so good for bullies, who are much more likely than their victims to drop out of school, get in trouble with the law, and suffer from serious mental illnesses, even long after their school-age bullying days are over. Victims do need support. They need help feeling better about themselves, feeling safe and actually being safe, and feeling that the school is theirs and they belong there. Bullies need other ways to feel important and valued besides lording it over other kids.

I always feel that punishments for bullies should involve time spent doing something socially constructive like painting No Bullying signs and posting them in the school, helping rake leaves on campus, or working with a community service group rather than sitting in detention.

I can see why you, as the parent of someone who is being victimized, have no tolerance for the administration of the school hiding behind arguments about bullies' low self-esteem. The Teasing and Bullying Task Force I worked with came up with a great question for the survey they conducted at their school. Since it can be hard to measure how badly a child is being teased or bullied, they asked kids whether they ever felt so badly teased or bullied that it interfered with their ability to learn. About 14 percent of the middle-schoolers said yes to that question. What made it a great question is that educators have to sit up and take notice when children tell them that social problems at the school are interfering with education.

I think the way for you to deal with the school is to focus on the impact of the bullying on your son's education, and the impact of the social climate of the school on every child's education. From that perspective, the self-esteem controversy isn't really relevant. What is relevant is the actual bullying behavior and its impact.

That approach also avoids another problem. School administrators sometimes have a tendency to downplay teasing and bullying on their campuses. They may resist calls to "do more" about bullying if they tend to think of parents as overly zealous protectors who are trying to give their own child special protection from the little bumps and bruises that are the inevitable parts of growing up. To avoid that perception, it will help to ask the teachers and administrators what they actually see going on at school and work to reconcile that with what you hear from your son.

Schools are also wary of trying to solve bullying problems simply by punishing the bully. They have learned the hard way that it isn't as simple as that. Punishment often just drives the behavior underground or sets the victims up for reprisals from the perpetrators for getting them in trouble. On the other hand, schools must take a strong moral stand against bullying and not turn a blind eye.

Interventions that really work at schools involve the whole system, at every level. That includes assemblies for the whole student body, training for teachers, meetings for parents, guidelines for classrooms, and well-established plans for handling bullies, victims, and the majority of children in between. And this systemwide approach can't just be a one-shot deal for a single school year. It has to be a real commitment.

Widening a Child's Social Circle

Q: *My seven-year-old daughter, Marian, has been friends with Heather since they were both three and in preschool together. They attended the same kindergarten and first grade* *classes, and during that time they were the very best of friends, almost inseparable. Now things have changed. Marian considers Heather one of her good friends—only one among four or five. The trouble is that Heather wants to have the same exclusive relationship that they had when they were five. This summer we were at the town pool and Marian had a family friend from out of town with her. Heather and her mother walked over to us to say hi, and as we started to introduce the new girl as a friend Heather put her hands over her ears, made a face, and shook her head. It was painful and embarrassing. She clearly did not want to meet or even acknowledge anyone else Marian considered a friend. I didn't know what to do! How should I handle things, both with Heather and with her mother? From this and other interactions, it's clear to me that Heather's mother also wants the girls' friendship to remain exclusive.*

A: What a painful and awkward scene! What makes it particularly difficult is that Heather acted like a four- or even three-year-old by throwing a minitantrum in public and trying to change reality through denial and wishes. I cannot help but be embarrassed for her and embarrassed for her mother. Apparently Heather's mom wasn't aware of how immature her daughter was in that moment. Or perhaps the mother covertly shares her daughter's anxiety about growing up and losing the cozy familiarity of the exclusive best friendship.

As children grow, friendships change. They evolve because children develop new abilities and interests. Old friends are often shed and discarded like the outgrown shell of a lobster, not because they are defective but because they do not fit so well anymore. It is a natural and inevitable process. Fighting it is futile. Children will be drawn to new people who seem a better fit for their developing interests and identities. Indeed, new friendships can be a signal that children are growing. Your daughter, Marian, is a healthy girl, and she's doing what she needs to do. She's not being cruel to Heather or betraying her. She is just growing up.

Heather's relationship with Marian is changing because Marian wants it to change. She no longer wants an exclusive relationship with Heather. Well, that's not a crime, even though it does leave Heather feeling hurt and betrayed. Heather hopes that through a combination of denial and public tantrum she can force Marian to relent and maintain an exclusive relationship with her. But it won't work. Indeed, the strategy she adopted at the pool was enough to drive away any friend.

Unfortunately, both Heather and her mother experience your daughter's growth as a rejection. I suspect that either Heather or her mother—or both—is anxious about her growing up. They have imagined that Heather's friendship with Marian would protect her from the rough-and-tumble of childhood relationships. The bond was supposed to be Heather's bulwark against hurt. Perhaps it fit with her mother's romantic ideal of what childhood friendship should be about.

Sometimes, if children are anxious about what is going to happen next, we try to protect them from inevitable losses by freezing their world. Sometimes, if parents are too anxious, we romanticize a particular thing in the child's life and try to keep it just the way it is. There is a trend among mothers that prompts them to come to their child's (usually their daughter's) school in June to try to influence the choice of teacher and classmates for the following year. They are prone to saying, "She just *has* to be with Sarah. Sarah is her best friend, and they would be desolate without each other." I think this type of intervention is unfortunate. Whenever I am addressing a group of mothers I ask them, "Would you have liked your mother to arrange who your best friend was going to be year after year?" When I ask in public, they say no. But some mothers insist on managing their children's friendships in just that way—and it's a mistake to try.

You were right to do nothing at the pool. Anything you said would have been humiliating. At some later point, however, you need to call Heather's mother and, without referring to the pool incident, say, "I know that Marian and Heather's relationship has changed somewhat. Is Heather handling it okay? Marian is worried about her but doesn't know how to talk to her about these things." Given that they are both seven years old, it is necessary for you and the other mother to be the ones to have a sensible conversation.

In the conversation all you have to do is advocate for the natural course of development and the principle of no coercion in friendship. Heather may try to manipulate her mom; all children do that to a certain extent. Don't get into that. Just point out that Marian likes Heather very much and always has, but that as she grows up she doesn't want just one exclusive relationship. Attribute it to your daughter's natural temperament; that gets everyone off the hook. And you can speak to Heather's desire to hold on to the exclusive friendship as a manifestation of her temperament. Don't call it anxiety, even though Heather is clearly anxious. Instead call it preference: "Right now Marion seems to want to have lots of friends, and Heather seems to want one really close one. That difference can be hard." And whatever you do, don't let

Heather's mom guilt you into agreeing that you will advocate for an exclusive relationship between the girls. Don't give in. Your daughter will be mad at you for allowing yourself to be manipulated. And it won't work. Your daughter is going to keep the friends she wants to keep, no matter what Heather and her mom want. Trying to stop that process is like trying to stop tulips from coming up in the spring. It can't be done. They spring up everywhere, as do the friendships of children.

When Other Families Don't Follow Your Rules

Q: *My daughter Lizzie has struck up a friendship with Kara, one of the most popular and powerful girls in her fourth-grade class. She's thrilled about it. But my husband and I are less than thrilled. The other girl's parents' values and parenting style are very different from ours. For example, Kara is allowed to watch anything she wants on TV, including* Friends *and other shows we consider too adult for fourth graders. There's also no set bedtime in her household. Lizzie feels that she has to go along with this girl's rules or risk losing her friendship and being teased for being babyish. I don't want to ruin things for her with her new friend, but I want to maintain our family rules about TV and bedtime. Is there anything I can do?*

A: There is a simple and straightforward solution to this problem, but almost no one uses it. Very few parents are willing to call the parents of their child's friends to discuss differences in parenting style. I think I understand why (more about that later), but for the sake of argument let me make the following proposal. Why don't you simply call the parents of Lizzie's new friend and say the following: "We're delighted with Lizzie's new friendship with Kara. Lizzie very much respects and admires her, and she is very excited to be invited for a sleepover at your house, but we have a couple of concerns we would like to run by you. We're quite strict about the things Lizzie watches on TV. We control things pretty tightly in our house, and we don't allow her to watch *Friends* because it is too focused on sex and it makes us uncomfortable to have Lizzie watch it. Would it be an imposition on you if we asked that they not be allowed to watch *Friends*? Our second concern is that Lizzie is simply horrible to be with if she hasn't had enough sleep. We have found that in the past when she's been on sleepovers, she is cranky and miserable all the next day. Would you make an attempt to get her into bed by ten-forty-five? I know that it can be tough to get kids to go to bed at a decent hour; however, we have to go to Lizzie's grandmother's the next day, and we would really appreciate it if she were rested."

Did reading that paragraph make you uncomfortable? Did you think, "Oh my God, I could never do that!" If so, then you, like many parents, are reluctant to call other families and lay out your worries. What are you scared will happen? Are you afraid that you will break up a budding friendship? I don't think that's likely, but I guess it's possible. The problem is that you clearly have reservations about this new friendship and you cannot hide that from Lizzie for long. My confident prediction is that you will "interfere" in some way, either overtly or covertly. If you don't make that call, you are very likely to employ sneaky methods that don't really address the problem.

If you are like many parents, you will instead resort to veiled warnings and disapproval of the new, cool friend. Lizzie will sense your attitude and heartily resent it. Children tell me that the one thing they hate the most is when parents disapprove of their friends. Your attitude of disapproval won't end the friendship, but it will drive a bit of a wedge between you and Lizzie. It might cause conflict in your house. Still, most parents would rather endure that conflict at home than make that telephone call. Why? What are parents so afraid of?

I think there are three reasons why parents don't want to talk to other parents about parenting. First, many of us in the United States don't live in communities that have common values. Particularly in the suburbs, we all live in our own castles, and we're not in the habit of discussing our parenting styles with the people up and down the street, or with the parents of our children's schoolmates. Indeed, to even discuss values with a stranger can feel un-American. It can feel like judging people, imposing values on them, or inviting public scrutiny of our own values. There is a cultural inhibition at work here, one that Robert Bellah described in his Pulitzer Prize–winning book, *Habits of the Heart.* He writes that American individualism trumps a sense of community most of the time. If Bellah is right, you don't want to appear to be challenging or questioning the values of Kara's family, because as Americans, we respect the right of each individual to hold to his or her own beliefs. So we don't want to appear to be questioning another family's *rights*. That would be socially unacceptable.

The second reason we don't make that call is because we know our children will be furious if we do. Children hate it when their parents call other parents because it makes them feel as if they are not autonomous creatures who roam the earth driven only by their own free will. Of course, they aren't. But they love to feel that they are. My daughter and a girlfriend once went over to a boy's house without telling us where they were. When I discovered this and asked her angrily why she hadn't given us the name and address of the boy, she said, "But Dad, you and Mom always call the parents when I'm going somewhere!" Yes, that's right. We almost always did when she was young, and we still do much of the time. Not always, not in every situation—and we might not have in that situation because she was going with a trusted friend—but we usually want to have contact with the parents of our children's friends. That is embarrassing to children. It makes them feel monitored and supervised. Right. That's exactly the feeling that I want my children to have. Not oppressed, mind you. I don't want my kids to feel squashed. However, I do want to know where they are, and I do want them to have the feeling that their mom and I, and our family's values, are present no matter where they are.

The third reason parents don't make that phone call is the most embarrassing one. Most of us don't want to admit that we feel this, but here it is: Making a phone call like that is *not cool*. Indeed, it is the opposite of cool. If you phone Kara's parents, you might as well hang a sign around your neck saying I Am a Total Dork. Here you are, calling the parents of the cool kid, and you have to admit that you don't let Lizzie watch cool TV? You're ready to admit that you think that getting sleep is more important than a brand-new friendship with a socially popular kid? Geek! Loser! Get a life!

You see, we all have a small part of us that remembers middle school and can still experience the feelings we felt in fifth grade. For most of us that means fearing the judgment of the cool group. Lizzie's friend Kara is at the center of the popular crowd. Her parents must be pretty cool, right? If we make that phone call, we're branding ourselves, and our child, as socially backward. That's a hard thing to do.

Yet one parent I know who made the kind of phone call I have proposed admitted she was surprised to have the other child's father say, "Oh, you don't let your daughter watch that show? Perhaps we shouldn't either." The other family was willing to model themselves on her! Has it occurred to you that perhaps Kara is boasting? Perhaps she doesn't stay up as late as she claims. Or perhaps she does it without her parents knowing. When you call, you will be subtly alerting them. Maybe she saw *Friends* once and has boasted about it for months afterward. You'll never know unless you make contact with her parents. It isn't a cool move, but I strongly doubt that Kara will hate Lizzie or Kara's parents will hate you if you make that call. I do predict that Lizzie will be mad at you for a short time. But she might just come back from her sleepover rested after having happily watched the Nickelodeon channel on TV.

When a Parent Doesn't Know How to Help

Q: *My sixth-grade daughter asked me a question I couldn't answer—something that happens more often now that she's in middle school. It seems that two groups of her friends got into a feud, and she thought both were wrong. Her question was, "Who do I sit with at lunch tomorrow?" I suggested inviting one girl from each group. After all, my daughter's not angry with anyone. She laughed at my naivete. "That wouldn't work," she said witheringly. "Whoever got there second would storm away!" I just didn't know what else to tell her. What could I have said?*

A: Your question is a lovely illustration of why parents usually cannot intervene effectively in a child's social life. There are very few parents (perhaps none at all) who would know what to tell their child in this situation. Many social problems that children face—moments of genuine social agony to them—are just too complex for a parent to unravel. This is one of those moments that falls into the category of unanswerable questions. All you can do when that happens is ask your daughter questions until she becomes exasperated with your stupidity.

The conversation might go something like this:

Daughter: Dad, I'm worried. I don't know who I can sit with at lunch tomorrow.
Father: Why not? Why can't you sit with anyone you want?

Daughter: Because all the girls are mad at each other. They're fighting.

Father: About what?

Daughter: Well, Kelly's group was dancing during recess and the other girls said, "You're stupid." They were really mean to the girls who were dancing. Kelly's dances were kind of wild and dumb and she wanted everyone to dance at recess, but they weren't *that* bad, and the girls who teased the girls who were dancing shouldn't have been so nasty. And so now they're not talking and I don't know who to sit with tomorrow.

Father: I know that Kelly is a good friend of yours. Maybe you should stick up for her for being teased.

Daughter: Normally I would, but after Tammy and the others teased the dancers, the dancers were really, really mean back. I mean nasty. So it's like if I side with anyone, I'm saying it's okay for them to be mean.

Father: Why don't you sit down first and just let someone sit down with you?

Daughter: But they won't know that I've gotten there first. The other group will think I've chosen sides.

Father: Well, why don't you just announce in public that you don't want to choose sides in the fight? Just tell everyone that you are friends with both sides and you want to be able to sit with everyone.

Daughter: Dad, if I made an announcement like that, it would make me look like I was trying to be better than everyone else. That would be weird. People would say that I was stuck up.

Father: Would you let that make you feel bad?

Daughter: I'd feel terrible.

Father: I have an idea. Why don't you just sit with someone from a totally different group? Just avoid the whole situation until things cool down.

Daughter: *Dad*, I'm not going to sit with a bunch of kids I hardly know!

Father: You know them. You've been going to school with them for years.

Daughter: But they're not my friends. I want to sit with my friends.

Father: But your friends are fighting and you're caught in the middle.

Daughter: I know that, Dad. I'm the one who told you that.

Father: I'm only trying to help!

Daughter: You're just being annoying, asking me all these questions.

Father: Well, don't you think this will all blow over in a couple of days? I mean, they can't keep this fight up too long, can they?

Daughter: Dad, they're really mad at each other. And I don't know who I can sit with tomorrow.

Father (feeling helpless): Well, I'm sure I don't know!

Daughter (feeling much better): You're no help at all!

This father has fallen into the classic parental trap of believing that he was actually being asked to suggest a solution to the problem. He was not. He was being asked to listen to a story and to absorb some of his child's sense of helplessness. If you were paying attention, you might have noticed that at the very beginning, she said she was "worried." She did not say she wanted a solution.

It is so uncomfortable for us to hear difficult stories from our children's lives, to hear that they are in pain in any way, that we find ourselves almost compelled to leap into problem-solving mode and offer them solutions. There are very few dedicated parents who can resist the temptation to do so. What is difficult to understand is that this father was being asked to appreciate the complexity of his daughter's social life, and the depth of her feelings, without getting involved.

Why do our children do this to us? They want us to know that they face real problems out there in life. They want us to know that their social lives are complex and demanding. They want us to appreciate that they struggle to find solutions. And they want someone to share their sense of helplessness about a situation. But they don't want us to come up with an answer, certainly not an easy or obvious one. If we were able to do that, it would make our children feel stupid and little.

The Power of Love

Q: *Last year I discovered that when my daughter, Sylvia, had been over at the home of her friend Joanne, the two of them had gone to the local drugstore and stolen candy. I was so outraged that I told Sylvia she couldn't see Joanne anymore. She couldn't go over to her house, nor could Joanne come to our house. That was close to a year ago. Since then, every week, without fail, Sylvia has asked me whether she can get together* *with Joanne again. They are together in school, and I think that's enough. Joanne is bad news. She's the kind of girl who in a few years will introduce Sylvia to smoking or encourage her to have sex. Joanne comes from an entirely different kind of family than ours. Since Sylvia is only nine years old, I expected that she would give up her friend after a couple of months. I am amazed that she is still under Joanne's spell. What can I do about Sylvia's attraction to someone who is a bad influence on her? When will she finally give up and make friends with other children?*

A: The problem you describe is a testament to the power of love. Children don't just like their friends a little bit, they love their friends. Moreover, your daughter is a very loyal person. As long as the girls live in the same town and go to the same school, I can't guarantee that Sylvia will ever give up her friendship with Joanne. Sylvia hasn't moved on to other friends because she really does love Joanne. It is a natural feeling, the result of the mystical chemistry between human beings. And there is almost nothing that we as parents can do about it. Psychologists know that children show strong preferences for certain other children in babyhood. As soon as they can crawl they seek out a favorite partner. You can force your daughter to give up visiting her friend, or ban her friend from your house, but there is no way you can successfully redirect Sylvia's affections. She is going to love the person she loves.

Parents are sometimes startled when I talk about love between children. They imagine that love is something that adults feel and that a child's version is milder or more diluted. They couldn't be further from the truth. Children love with all their might. We discount their affections at our, and their, peril. Why do I say that? Let me give you an example. Perhaps the most loving person on earth is the toddler who throws a tantrum, cries, and pleads, "Don't leave me," when his mother is going out for the evening and leaving him with a baby-sitter. Overwhelmed and disconsolate at the idea of losing his most precious person, he fights a noble fight. A three-year-old loves his mother with all the intensity he has. He is filled with as much desperation and longing as a lover of any age. The same is true of a twelve-year-old who has a best friend, or a seventeen-year-old who is experiencing romantic love for the first time. Remember that Romeo and Juliet were teenagers. And so it is that Sylvia, age nine, can carry the torch for her friend for more than a year. If you are thinking that you can wait her out, you are likely to be in for a surprise.

The hard part for parents is that they think their children *shouldn't* be that attached to anyone outside the family at so early an age. They believe that children should love Mom and Dad best. And, of course, children do. But even though parents are at the center of their children's affections, there is plenty of room for others: for brothers and sisters, for grandparents, for friends. As parents, we also believe that we should be the dominant influence on our children's growth and especially their moral behavior. That's why you found Sylvia's candy theft so upsetting. I understand your impulse to keep Sylvia away from Joanne, but I believe it is a mistake to do so. And it is not just an ordinary mistake; it is a serious mistake.

Given Sylvia's fierce loyalty to Joanne, why would you want to make a fight of it? Why would you force her to choose between you and her friend? Why would you want your daughter to think of you as the enemy of her friends? That isn't the view that you want Sylvia to have of you in years to come. I have had many adult patients tell me how much they hated it when their parents opposed their friendships or said critical things about their friends. You might argue with me, saying that Joanne is a bad influence on Sylvia and has led her down the wrong path. But do you really think Sylvia is just a follower? Is Joanne the only one of the pair who has any risk-taking impulses? Perhaps they encouraged each other to steal. Perhaps they were both excited by the idea of having that candy. It's one-sided to think that only Joanne could think up an exploit like that. Didn't you ever do anything bad behind your mother's back? If you never did, you're in a small minority. Most kids feel a need to push limits, to break the rules, and so they disobey their parents from time to time. That is part of growing up. And they usually do it with a friend. That is—in one sense—what friends are for, (Of course, friends can also help check each other from getting carried too far into risky behavior.)

The solution to your problem is for you to invite Joanne over to your house and supervise the girls' friendship. You can decide whether or not they go to the store, or you can go with them. Spend enough time with Joanne so that *you* start to like her, or at least to understand why Sylvia likes her so much. Watch the affection between them. Delight in it. Someone loves your daughter. That is what we all want for our children.

If, as I suspect, your daughter's friend is from a different socioeconomic background than yours, I suggest that you make an effort to get to know her mother. Invite her for coffee when she comes to pick up Joanne from your house. Talk to her long enough to feel comfortable with her, to develop enough ease to tell her some of your worries about the friendship. Be careful not to blame her daughter for the girls' misbehavior. I want you to be able to say to her, "When our girls get together, they like getting into trouble. I have to keep an eye on them." You may be surprised by what the other mom says. She's likely to tell you that she caught them doing something too. Perhaps, in her mind, your daughter was the leader and Joanne a follower in their troublemaking.

If you and Joanne's mother start to have a bit of a relationship, you will be able to talk with one another and to take pleasure in the girls' love and loyalty for each other. And you can both keep an eye out for trouble! It will be less lonely for you if you can make an ally out of Joanne's mother. And Sylvia will be grateful to you for allowing her to pursue her friendship with her beloved friend. In the end, your worry about bad influences must take a back seat to the importance of supporting the friendships your daughter chooses.

The Language of Put-downs

Q: *Ever since my son started middle school, he and his friends seem to be in a constant state of verbal warfare. They talk almost entirely in put-downs and insults, whether they are talking to their best friend or someone they don't like at all. If I* *dare to suggest that they speak nicely to one another, they look at me as if I have two heads. Why do middle-school students, especially boys, put each other down so much?*

A: For many children, but especially middle-school boys, put-downs are part of the culture. They are a language, even an art form. Insults and swear words can express almost every mood and emotion, from hostility to casual greeting to affection. It can be hard for an outsider—especially an adult—to untangle the meaning and purpose of the put-down in any particular interaction.

The language of put-downs and insults has been passed down from generation to generation of children and adolescents, just like the rules to playground games. The specific words may change over time, but the purpose of the language remains the same: to shock adults, to proclaim your identity as a teenager, to one-up your peers, and to express yourself.

In recent years, as a result of the modeling of television and movies and popular music, where super-hip, precocious kids talk in put-downs to peers and to adults, and adults speak this language to one another, it has become more acceptable to use put-downs to communicate in public. Cynicism, criticism, and negativity are pervasive at almost every level of our culture.

Children tend to pass on to other children any type of abuse they experience themselves. So if they are hit at home, they might hit smaller children. If they are called names at home or on the street, they may call other children names.

People who are members of groups that have been oppressed and mistreated by society often adopt the epithets and insults that have been targeted at them. White people are often shocked when black kids call each other "nigger," but this usage can be seen as a way of defusing the insult by adopting it. However, it is also a sign of internalizing racism by taking what was targeted at the group and aiming it at one another. I have seen the same phenomenon with gay men calling each other "fag" or "homo," Jews telling jokes about JAPs (Jewish-American princesses), and so on.

Put-downs are appealing to many children because they are at the same time the language of the in-group and the language of alienation. One of the uses of put-downs that confuses adults or outsiders is as expressions of affection and friendship. This happens especially among boys because the pressure to look cool—and to avoid looking homosexual—prevents direct expressions of affection or appreciation between boys. So boys mask their true feelings of tenderness and affection for one another with punches and put-downs.

Of course, put-downs are also an expression of hostility, prejudice, or intolerance. There may be only subtle differences between the way an obscene taunt is used with an enemy and the way the same words are used with a friend.

Verbal prowess, especially in dishing out insults, is used to establish the dominance hierarchy. Often this is an alternative to physical fighting, the same way that some animals will use behavioral displays to assert their superiority until someone backs down. Boys use this kind of verbal sparring to test each other's mettle. The purpose isn't just to see who is the alpha male but to broadly distinguish the ones who can take the abuse from the ones who can't. The latter group may be targeted later with a specific set of insults (crybabies, sissies) or they may be seen as easy prey for aggressive or sadistic boys.

Middle school is a time of enforced conformity to group norms. Any type of deviance from these norms, whether of dress, behavior, speech, or taste in music and movies, is instantly and often harshly punished. The punishments take many forms, with girls often preferring gossip and subtle (or not so subtle) exclusion of the girl who violates the norms, while boys often prefer to directly target the rule breaker with verbal or physical aggression. This is especially true for violations of the norms of masculinity, such as crying or being a goody-goody.

I hope this helps to illuminate some of the varied reasons why children—more frequently boys—talk to each other in put-downs. I hope it also provides some direction about whether or not you should be concerned about your own child's use of this language.

Saying Good-bye to School

Q: *I am the principal of a suburban high school. Every spring—no matter what I do to try to prevent it—the seniors start acting up. It isn't just spring fever. They insist that they hate the school and can't wait to leave. Some of them seem to be trying their hardest to be thrown out of school right before they graduate! Then when they come back to visit they can't find enough good things to say about their time here. What's going on?*

A: If you talked to the principal of an elementary or middle school, you would find out that your colleagues face a version of this kind of spring madness with their oldest students, too. When it's getting close to time for kids to say good-bye to a familiar part of their world, they often begin to behave badly. Maybe saying they don't want to be there anymore makes it a little easier to go.

Graduation means moving on, but it also means letting go of significant attachments. When you hear a psychologist talk about attachment, you probably think about small children—infants, toddlers, maybe preschoolers. But attachment is a key issue for people of all ages, and attachment is the issue, I think, for your seniors.

Whenever there is a strong attachment—a bond between people, a connection, a feeling of belonging—there is also the potential for loss. And so no matter how excited seniors may be to be graduating, leaving high school is a huge loss. They are losing the familiar, of course, but most importantly they face the loss of a circle of friends, a peer group, a class, a school identity, and perhaps the loss of a team that they joined as a lowly freshman and are leaving as a lordly senior. Or they are facing the loss of a drama club, a chess club, a group to hang out with, maybe even a favorite teacher.

Even if some of the seniors hated their classes, hated the teachers, or hated the principal (sorry!), leaving school is still a loss. School has been their second home for years. They might insist that there is no loss involved, and you might even wonder how they could be feeling loss when you can't wait for them to leave, but rest assured that the loss is very real. How can it be a loss to leave something they hate? I'm not sure exactly how this works, but I know it's always true. Consider children who are taken away from their homes and placed in foster care because of severe abuse and neglect: They may be glad to be in a safe environment, but they *always* feel a huge sense of loss.

Of course, your high school is not a place of abuse and neglect. For almost all the seniors there, it has been a place of joy and growth and camaraderie—at least some of the time. And for most of them, most of the time, school has been a place where they show up five days a week primarily to spend hours with their friends and companions. So the loss that is impending for these children is enormous.

And what do human beings do when they are facing a loss? We learned about this years ago, when Dr. Elisabeth Kübler-Ross first studied the grieving process. We deny the loss and rage against it before we ever get around to accepting it. Your seniors are not going to spend the three months before graduation weeping or admitting to being scared of what's coming next in their lives. If they survive to graduation day without being expelled—and of course most of them do—then they will probably do some crying then. And they will probably tell you and their teachers and their parents how much they loved the old place.

But before graduation, they act their feelings out instead. "Acting out" simply means that a person takes some action, often a destructive one, so that the feelings underneath don't have to be faced, felt, and (God forbid) released in tears or trembling. The opposite of acting out isn't "behaving," but rather acknowledging the feelings of loss and fear.

So is it any wonder that it's the boys who are usually

most involved with the kinds of acting out and graduation panic that I am describing? Prohibited by the rules of manhood from crying or even talking about how they feel, they have to do *something* with those feelings. And that something is generally something adults hate. When a group of adolescents gets together and they all are experiencing buried feelings of impending loss, the risk taking and rule bending gets amplified even more. (See "When the Group Causes Trouble," page 69.) Add the fact that the group is lurching toward adulthood and experimenting with independence— and often with alcohol, sex, and drugs as well. During this experimentation they have a tendency to "crash and burn" as they approach graduation and the upcoming change in structure and limits. No self-respecting teenager ever asks for *more* structure or limits, but through their acting out they are in a way announcing that they aren't sure whether they are quite ready for independence.

Walking on thin ice about being expelled is another part of this process of attachment and loss. I think it's a variation of "You can't fire me! I quit," or "I'll break up with you before you break up with me." If you can't admit how much you care, it may seem that the best tactic is to show that you don't care at all.

Anyone who has ever worked in a psychiatric hospital has seen this phenomenon over and over again. Most escapes from locked wards happen shortly before a patient was about to be released anyway. They may have been saying for months that they can't wait to leave, and they know that an escape will result in being brought back for an even longer stay. But the pressure builds up and the impulse to run is uncontrollable. The combination of fear of the real world after their discharge and the loss of the familiar world of the hospital—hated, perhaps, but still familiar—combine to overwhelm the patient.

Of course, your students are not inmates of a mental institution, even though some say that adolescence is a temporary form of insanity. But the process of attachment and loss can look very similar.

Does it help to know that all this acting out means that your seniors really love the school with all their hearts and are very sad to be leaving? No? I was afraid of that. But it's true, and maybe keeping that thought in mind will help a little bit in the long run. After all, you're facing a loss, too, as this year's senior class gets ready to go.

The Kindness of Children

Q: *My son, who is eleven, has wonderful friends. They call each other by affectionate nicknames like "Bubba." They can't wait to see each other or call each other. They are respectful of the others when they have sleepovers, and they take turns playing computer games. They remember each other's birthdays and want to buy each other nice presents. But if you listen to the "experts" who write about boys, everything is about anger, violence, and bullying. They never seem to say anything about the close friendships that exist between boys—or between girls, for that matter! My older daughter has long-standing affectionate relationships as well. Will my son and his friends lose their respect and affection for one another as they grow into adolescence? Will they become more distant or turn into bullies?*

A: There is no reason why your children should have to lose their friendships as they grow. Nor is there any reason why they should have to become bullies. Indeed, the fact that they have had such good friendships means that they will be able to stay close to their friends and to back one another up.

There are many grown men and women whose friendships have lasted for years and years. I have often polled audiences about their childhood friendships, and about fifteen percent of people raise their hands when I ask if they have a close, continuous friendship that dates back to before second grade. My elderly neighbor, at age eighty-eight, came out of her front door one day to tell me that she was grief-stricken because her best friend from kindergarten had just died. They had enjoyed an eighty-three-year friendship.

You are absolutely right about experts tending to concentrate too much on the negative—including the authors of this book. The intensity of the pain and suffering and cruelty experienced by some children, and the anxiety of their parents, can indeed blind us to the incredible friendliness and compassion that young people show one another every single day. Children light up when they see their friends, and they walk with their heads held high when they know they have a solid place in the group.

Just the other day a friend of mine told me he was so proud when he saw his daughter writing a letter to a friend whom she sees in school every day. He asked her what she was doing, and she said her friend Molly was upset because she never got any personal mail. So his daughter wrote her a letter. The letter was funny. It pretended to be from a little old lady who had been observing Molly and had noticed all kinds of wonderful things about her. Then at the end his daughter revealed that it was really from her. When Molly got the letter she called and said that it had "made her decade," which is pretty good coming from an eleven-year-old.

There are a million stories like this repeated every day. Some are poignant, like the boy who entered the Run for Hunger race on behalf of his friend who was injured in a car crash. Others are inspiring, like the classroom where no one teases or excludes the boy with cerebral palsy. Some stories can't help but make us smile, like the varsity football team who all show up on opening night, looking very itchy and a little uncomfortable in their pressed clothes, to see their teammate perform in an opera, the only thing he loves more than football. And some are sweet, like the boy who tried to convince his mother that a sleepover with his best friend would not be an added burden right before the holidays. "We're really almost like one person, Mom," he said. "We'll use one plate and one fork at dinner, and we'll even let my little sister pick what movie to watch."

This question is a great place for me to make a plug for one of my favorite books about children's social lives. It was written by Vivian Paley, a retired kindergarten teacher and a beautiful storyteller who has been an inspiration to us and to countless teachers and parents as well. In *The Kindness of Children,* Paley goes against the idea that children are uniquely and inevitably cruel, and encourages teachers to expect kindness and compassion from children.

In our own previous book, *Best Friends, Worst Enemies,* we said that any adult can think back to seventh grade and recall who was popular and who was unpopular, and those haunting memories will come racing back. But it's also true that if you ask an adult what his or her best memories of childhood are, they will almost always mention a moment with a friend or a group of friends. Most days children don't come running home crying, "Mom, they're teasing me!" Instead they come home saying, "I made a new friend," or "I made the team," or "Can I go over to Jimmy's right away?" Or better yet, they don't tell us anything, but we hear them giggling away with their friends or see them, heads bent, concentrating together on a new game. We can feel the bonds that link them with the other children they care about so deeply.